"The informatic
munities and th
develop them is most informat
on cultivating dynamic learning cultures. I believe that Head-masters, Principals, and others tasked with leading teams in education institutions would benefit from this book."

Nick Miller, Ph.D., Headmaster

"Chuck provides excellent food for thought for executive search consultants and anyone serving on search committees. He presents a strong case for seeking attributes that we would want in any leader of an institution that serves society; and, he provokes careful examination of those leadership qualities."

Edith Soares, Executive Search Consultant (Retired)

"I have had the opportunity to know many leaders in the NGO, business, and government sectors in Hong Kong and China. Chuck Allison is one such leader. He identifies attributes that ensure integrity in leaders and in organization. His chapter on practices and tools has insights that CEOs will find invaluable. Every chapter illustrates points about leadership, and the character it demands to be truly successful."

Cheung-Ang Siew Mei, JP, CEO of Christian Action

[*Christian Action is a non-profit, charitable organization dedicated to improving conditions for the poor, marginalized, and abandoned in Hong Kong and China.*]

"While written from his experience in the social sector, the information that Chuck presents is equally applicable to leaders in the business sector. Indeed, those called to leadership in every walk of life and work will benefit from this book."

Bob Burnham, Entrepreneur and
Author of several #1 Amazon Best Sellers

May your work be a blessing to others.

Blessings & Peace

Chuck

LEADERSHIP
in Social Sector Institutions

Examining
4 Essential Attributes
in Leaders

———•———

Featuring 3 Stories on Life and Vocation:

*The Wandering, Miracle,
& The Three Stewards Plan*

Chuck Allison

Copyright © 2014 Chuck Allison
All rights reserved.
Unauthorized duplication or distribution is strictly prohibited.

ISBN 13 - 978-0-9912964-6-0
ISBN 10 - 099129646X

Published by: Expert Author Publishing
http://expertauthorpublishing.com

Canadian Address:
1265 Charter Hill Drive
Coquitlam, BC, V3E 1P1
Phone: (604) 941-3041
Fax: (604) 944-7993

US Address:
1300 Boblett Street
Unit A-218
Blaine, WA 98230
Phone: (866) 492-6623
Fax: (250) 493-6603

Table of Contents

Acknowledgements vii
Foreword.................................... ix
Introduction xi

Life & Vocation Stories & Lessons *1*
Prologue – The Searcher 3
Story - The Wandering.........................5
Epilogue – In Search of Character 33
Questions for Reflection and Follow-up Study.........39

Prologue – Courage to Answer a Call 41
Story - Miracle................................43
Epilogue – In Search of Courage and Calling 73
Questions for Reflection and Further Study...........83

Prologue – A Mantra for Servant-Leaders 85
Story - The Three Stewards Plan...................87
Epilogue – Capability – The Essential Attribute for
Accepted Leadership............................105
Questions for Reflection and Further Study..........113

Summary, Practices & Tools, and References *115*
Summing up the Stories and the Search for the Four
Essential Attributes of Successful Social Sector Leaders. .117
Practices and Tools to Help Leaders Identify and Develop
Character, Courage, Calling and Competency, and
Cultivate Learning Organizations 121
Books and Work by Scholars Referenced 139

Acknowledgements

I want to publically thank those who read my draft manuscripts and offered comments that shaped the structure and content of the book, and made correction to its grammar and readability. These helpers include my wife Jackie and sister-in-law Janet, and other friends and family.

I appreciate that Bart Shaha offered to write the foreword for this book. As a published writer of books and music, he also gave me invaluable comments for effectively communicating the intended messages and lessons. As a former Secretary General of the World Alliance of YMCAs and head of one of the largest non-profit, charitable organizations in the world today, his comments on leadership not only add credibility to my words but add to the content of the book as a base document for aspiring young leaders in social sector institutions.

I give thanks for accomplished professionals like Siew Mei Ang-Cheung, Edith Soares, and Nick Miller who took the time to read the manuscript, and offer their insights and endorsement; and, to Bob Burnham for his expert guidance on writing and publishing.

It is my prayer that leaders of social sector institutions will be inspired to seriously recommit their energy and talent to the ongoing process of character and leadership development. The world sorely needs more leaders of integrity who strive for peace and justice in society. Efforts to develop righteous character and courageous, capable, and ethical leadership are essential in this quest.

Foreword

In this book Chuck Allison very creatively examines four essential attributes in leadership for social sector institutions. He identifies these attributes as: Character, Courage, Calling, and Capability. Instead of expounding directly on each of these attributes, which would probably be quite dry and strictly academic, he eloquently narrates three interesting *stories* portraying vividly the key characteristics of the identified attributes.

He also helps the reader to reflect upon and internalize the underlying messages and lessons from the stories by providing a brief Prologue, an Epilogue, and reflective questions before and after each of the stories. Thereafter, the four essential attributes are reviewed again through a careful summation, reminding the reader about the validity and importance of those attributes.

The book concludes with significant recommendations and tools to assist leaders identify and cultivate the essential attributes, derived from the author's meticulous study of contemporary theories on leadership and long professional experiences as a Chief Executive Officer (CEO) of an internationally renowned not-for-profit social organization.

I have known Chuck Allison since the early 1980s when he first moved to Hong Kong from Canada to serve as the CEO of the YMCA of Hong Kong with its headquarters located on Salisbury Road in Tsim Sha Tsui, overlooking the busy harbour of that vibrant and ever growing city. I was then serving as the Executive for Leadership Development of the Asia Alliance of YMCAs, the regional headquarters of the YMCAs in Asia and Pacific.

Since then, I have seen how Chuck has successfully given leadership to that YMCA expanding its programs in numerous multi-dimensional socio-cultural, spiritual, education, sports, games, and recreational activities. Through his vision and deep commitment to the Mission of the YMCA, he has been able to lead that YMCA movement to new horizons.

Much of what he shares in this book comes from his over 30 years' experience as a YMCA Professional Executive with immense international understanding, having worked with people of different religions, cultures, and nationalities.

This book is sure to inspire anyone wanting to pursue leadership with humility and passion in building a viable and ethical social organization responding to the needs of society.

Bartholomew Shaha, Ph.D.
Former Secretary General of the
World Alliance of YMCAs

Introduction

———◆———

As a 19 year old I went through a recruitment process for entry into the officer-training program in the Canadian military. I recall some military veterans in our community saying such things as, "They'll make a man out of you" or "They will make a leader out of you." I am sure that those gentlemen gave such comments to encourage me; and, perhaps also to forewarn me of the mental and physical testing that was to come in the recruit camp phase of the training. In any case, those comments of "making leaders" stuck in my mind as I stepped on an airplane for the first time and made the 3000-mile trip to military college.

Although the recruitment process was rigorous and thorough, I saw about a third of my peers leave the program by the end of the three-month compulsory stay. I was not aware upon arrival that those first few weeks were intended as a "recruit purging." I quickly realized that I needed to understand the rules if I was to play the game well. I was much too engaged in the process then to be concerned with longer-term learning but something must have been stored in the memory banks as those experiences would prove useful in various leadership roles that I was privileged to undertake in my career in the social service sector, including twenty-seven years as a CEO in the YMCA.

My perspectives on developing leadership have been shaped by a lifetime of personal experiences played out in the various arenas life has afforded. Those perspectives, and the art and science of developing leaders continue to evolve, as they should. Yet, it is my hope and prayer that the foundational perspectives that I share in this book will significantly help those responsible to build strong, effective, ethical, and sustainable organizations through the quality of their leaders.

Along with perspective, I will provide practical information that will allow leaders to leverage on their human resources to advance mission and stewardship within their organizations. When applied consistently, the practices that I lay out will ensure that an organization adds to its effectiveness in mission, and its reputation. These practical "tips" will not only provide tools that leaders can use to succeed but will also help them avoid pain and grief.

Grief avoidance is too polite a term in real life. Indeed, when leaders of organizations fail to manage affairs professionally and somehow make room for grief and despair to enter in, it will surely find a way to prosper – and that time will be very painful and hurtful. When this occurs, and it is usually unintended, it negatively impacts the organization as an entity, hurts its stakeholders and mission, and diminishes the reputation of its leaders, who are duty bound to be good stewards of its resources. While I prefer the grief components not dominate the messages contained in this book, leaders should always be aware that there are very real risks of grief occurring when the "right way" is not followed.

I will present basic knowledge of developing leadership in organizations by commenting on realistic life and work situations. The reading includes three fictitious short stories that were inspired by true events. I trust that the stories will catch your interest, as the **four essential attributes of leaders** are made visible therein.

The brief prologue to each of these stories will provide the reader with a sense of direction for their search and examination of the essential attributes of a leader. The lengthier epilogue and reflective questions will expound on these leadership attributes and position the reader to benefit from the practical recommendations that I provide in the last chapter.

It is no secret that I want you to look for the appearance of the four essential attributes of social sector leaders in the stories; i.e. Character, Courage, Calling, and Capability. I pray that when reading you will gain insight and inspiration for your work.

I anticipate your desire and commend your efforts to build social institutions that are financially viable, ethical, and effective in mission. I trust that you consider the messages contained herein carefully and prayerfully and determine to find, measure, nurture, and reward the four essential attributes in each and every leader at any level throughout your organization.

Chuck Allison

Life & Vocation
Stories & Lessons

Prologue - The Searcher

―――――♦―――――

" Besides being wise himself, the Searcher also taught others knowledge. He weighted, examined, and arranged many proverbs. The Searcher did his best to find the right words and write the plain truth.

The words of the wise prod us to live well.
They're like nails hammered home, holding life together.
They are given by God, the one Shepherd.

But regarding anything beyond this, dear friend, go easy.
There's no end to the publishing of books, and constant study wears you out so you're no good for anything else.
The last and final word is this:
Fear God. Do what he tells you. And that's it."

Ecclesiastes 12: 9 to 13
(The Message)

"Nearly all men can stand adversity,
but if you want to test a man's character, give him power."

Abraham Lincoln

Story -
The Wandering

John was delighted that his family had surprised him on his nineteenth birthday with a special party. It was a wonderful evening that would be etched in his memory for a lifetime – but its success was very touch and go and it almost didn't happen at all.

John's younger sister Sophia had instigated the plan. She collaborated with her parents to organize a fun-filled event with family and friends, three days prior to brother John's actual birthday. The family had a well-established tradition of making a big deal of birthday celebrations so timing the special event in advance of John's actual birthday may just keep it a surprise. Of course, many other details would need to be considered to keep it top secret.

Sophia and John were close in age and relationship. Only fifteen months separated their ages and they considered themselves kindred spirits. She was energized at the thought of organizing what was likely a once-in-a-lifetime party for her brother.

Sophia started making notes. One risk to the plan's success was that John had just started his university studies a few months earlier. The university was only a 30-minute drive from home but John chose to live in residence rather than commute. It was the best decision for John but did present another variable for Sophia to consider as he normally stayed on campus over weekends to train, study, and socialize – and hopefully in that order. John had earned a spot on the varsity basketball team. It was not a small thing for a freshman to win a position with the starting five and he was determined to keep it. That meant committing extra time to train on weekends. Mid-term exams were approaching as well. As Sophia considered all these variables, she worried that perhaps her surprise party idea might be a little too ambitious. "Maybe I've bitten off more than I can chew," Sophia muttered to herself head in hands.

Sophia got up from her desk, stretched her hands toward the ceiling, and took a few deep breaths to collect her confidence. She then sat down and opened her notebook again feverishly listing everything that needed to be done. "To succeed, nothing can be left to chance," Sophia reasoned in her thoughts now full of optimism.

Sophia had made an initial investigation and determined that John would not have any reason not to come home Friday afternoon. She had checked his basketball game schedule and noted there was not a game on that weekend. A phone call to Coach Bell proved very encouraging. "I decided to give the team the weekend off so they could prepare for the winter semester mid-term exams," he explained to Sophia. "Of course, they have all been given strict orders to complete their off-court exercises each day and…"

Sophia apologized and interrupted the conversation knowing that Coach was super enthusiastic about his team's development and had a tendency to ramble on with basketball talk. "Coach Bell, our family would be delighted if you could join us at the party," she injected with sincerity as it was true that everyone respected Coach.

He accepted. Sophia quickly added, "Don't mention a word. It is top secret."

"My lips are sealed," said Coach as the conversation came to an end.

Sophia now had enough information to form a plan outline. She would get John to go to a movie with her then afterward she would suggest grabbing something to eat, which of course would actually be his surprise party. She knew that John didn't have any reasonable excuse to turn her down for a movie date.

Sophia phoned her brother. John answered and following cordial brother-sister chitchat Sophia popped the question about the movie date. John replied, "I'd be happy to go to a movie with you Sophia," then hurriedly cut the conversation short with, "Oh, sorry, got to run now. Bye. Talk to you later. Text me the details." Sophia heard the call disconnect. She was a bit concerned about the abrupt end to the call but reasoned that John was very busy. She paused a moment and breathed easy with the knowledge that John did commit to go with her to a movie. However, she wasn't completely at peace. Something was unsettling her in her spirit.

A risk with any surprise party is, of course, that any one of the guests may leak information. John and most of his friends were avid social domain users. That added to the immensity of the confidentiality challenge. However, Sophia was just the person for the task. Her attention to detail, her disciplined approach to projects, and her excellent relational skills were put on full alert. Even her parents were amazed at the blanket of security that she laid over the event. "No texting or email, no writing down details, no loose lips," she told every invitee over the phone. Hearing the security protocol rapidly rhymed off elicited smiles and chuckles from each of the invitees.

As preparations moved into high gear a few days before the party, John called his sister with a concern about his availability. "Sophia, I am sorry but I want to ask you to postpone our movie. Some of the guys are going to the pub on Friday night and I said I'd join them," he said nonchalantly.

Sophia was deflated and responded with unusual haste and emotion, "But John, you had a date with me on Friday!"

There was an uncomfortable pause in the conversation. John was taken aback that his sister replied in a tone that communicated genuine hurt.

He responded rather sheepishly, "I know Sophia but I thought that we could reschedule. It's ... "

"Reschedule, reschedule," Sophia retorted. "I bet some of your basketball teammates put you up to this. That's not fair," Sophia continued.

"Wait, wait," said John. "No, it was not any of my basketball buddies. Just a few dorm mates."

At this point Sophia hung up the phone. John was shaken and unsure how to respond to his sister. He decided to go outside to shoot some hoops.

After collecting herself Sophia thought for a few minutes. She recalled that during her brief and emotionally charged conversation that he had said that nobody from the basketball team had been involved in the plans to go pubbing on Friday evening. Then an idea came to mind. "I'll call John's best friend on the basketball team and enlist his support to convince John to change his mind. This will have to be done tactfully so that John will not suspect an ulterior motive," she whispered to herself. So, with the surprise party on the verge of collapse, Sophia got on the phone once again.

Sophia had been introduced to Howard a few weeks earlier after a home basketball game. She observed that John and Howard were good friends and that John respected him. Coach Bell had a practice of coupling a mature junior or senior year player with a freshman. Howard was assigned to mentor John and the two of them were also roommates on road trips and tournaments. It was clear to her that they had a kinship and she discerned that Howard was a trustworthy person.

Howard wasn't startled when he looked at his call display that indicated that Sophia was calling. He reasoned that she wanted him to help somehow with John's surprise birthday party. He couldn't resist putting Sophia off-pace so he touched the green button and said, "Hi Sophia, are you calling to confirm our date Friday evening?" He thought his tactic worked, as there was silence at the other end of the phone. He was feeling pleased with himself as Sophia begin to speak. However, Howard realized from the tone of her voice that she was very upset and his jovial feeling vanished.

She explained that John had made different plans for Friday night. Sophia shared that it was very unlike John to change a date with her, particularly on such short notice and without consulting her. Sophia went on to explain that she and John had enjoyed a close, loving, and respectful relationship since childhood and she wouldn't have expected him to be so frivolous when changing plans like that. "Perhaps he has a serious girlfriend or some other secret he is withholding from me," she added, "It's Wednesday afternoon already and so many guests are coming…"

Howard could sense her emotion was rising so he gently interrupted Sophia's list of concerns and said, "Ok Sophia, let's discuss how to we get John back to the game plan?"

Howard's can-do comment and tone gave Sophia assurance that they could get the plan back on track. She settled into calm and soon she and Howard were having fun discussing ideas. A plan materialized and Sophia felt peace for the first time since she had hung up the phone on her brother. She was hopeful that Howard would be able to persuade John to spend Friday night at a movie and then be surprised at his party!

Howard and John met every Thursday morning for one

of the three strength-training sessions that Coach Bell had prescribed. Coach had them on an honour system to train on their own timetable. Players scheduled their own sessions so as not to conflict with academic timetables. Coincidently four other players on the team worked out at the same time on Thursdays.

Just before they entered the sports complex Howard asked John if he would join him and other basketball team members to watch a movie at the theatre house in town. He added that it was something the senior guys wanted to do and, while it was short-notice, there was a movie that just seemed to fit the bill. "It is about a woman boxer who gets a second chance at going pro at age 31," he said. "Even though it isn't about basketball Coach Bell thought it would be inspirational and good for team building."

Howard further explained that it was optional but so far all the players on the team were joining. "We plan to meet at the theatre at 5:15 for the 5:30 showing," Howard noted, "And, you and I can catch a ride with Eddie."

Howard was taken aback by John's silence that moments later erupted into a violent retort, "Sophia has put you up to this. I know she has!" Howard was dumbfounded by John's response. He could see that John's face was distorted and his rage was building.

John then yelled, "I don't believe other players are going. It is just a ploy to get me to go to the movies with my sister."

Upon hearing the ruckus, the other basketball teammates stopped getting dressed for their gym workout and joined Howard and John. John was throwing his shoes and cloths into the locker and causing quite a scene. One of the players in the locker room named Skip, who was a giant of a man, who appropriately played centre on the team, decided to calm things down. "Hey man," he said to John. "What's all this racket about?"

John turned away, then reversed and retorted sarcastically, "And I bet you are going to see the movie tomorrow with the rest of the team."

John looked intensely at Skip to observe his reaction. Skip had fifty pounds of muscle on John yet reason had vanished in John's state of rage. Skip was incensed but kept his calm. After a short pause, he smiled and replied in cool fashion, "Well, yah. Coach thought it was a good idea." He then looked around at the others and quipped, "And it's not like I have a lot else to do."

The other teammates were chuckling when Skip concluded, "So doing a movie with this mob is ok with me." He turned and gave Eddie a punch on the shoulder.

"Yah, I'm in too," Eddie shot back, "And it's about women boxers, what could be better?" The other guys were enjoying the exchange. Skip and Eddie were well known as team clowns but they had also hit the mark as good actors in this case. John's red face gave evidence that he was now convinced by the story line of a team-building movie. He felt stupid that he had shown such emotion in front of his senior teammates but he wasn't ready to apologize. He just remained silent.

"Anyway, now that you guys have shut up, let's go for a workout," Skip interjected, "Coach will be checking the log to see if we punched in on time." Everyone except John thought the comment funny as they all headed to the weight room.

It was a quiet workout. John wasn't in a talking mood and just focused on pushing weights and finishing his routine. Howard likewise worked through the routine of the exercises in relative silence with his teammate, not wanting to push the envelope and mention the topic of the movie again. The session came to an end. The men timed out and headed to the locker room. John suddenly turned around and faced Howard. "I'm sorry for all the fuss," he said. Howard remained silent to give John space. John then explained, "You see, I had promised Sophia that I'd go to a movie with her then I broke my promise and decided to go to the pub with some dorm mates." He muttered ashamedly, "I guess that I was more upset with her reaction than I thought."

Howard broke the tension with some humour, "It's tough when you are so popular. Let's hit the showers and think about how to get you out of your messy situation."

As John was putting on his jacket, he said to Howard, "I'm not sure what movie Sophia wanted to watch but would it be alright if she joined us. That way I can at least keep her happy – after I apologize of course."

Skip overheard and ruled in a macho voice, "Of course, your sister is always welcome."

The guys stood ready for Skip to receive a few punches but then noticed a smile slowly return to John's face.

"It's settled then," said Howard, "We'll all meet at the theatre ticket counter by 5:15."

All nodded and shuffled out of the locker room.

As they were heading their separate ways John yelled to Skip, "I'll get you later."

The giant smiled and headed to his next class. It seemed that the crisis was over – but there was no time to relax.

Howard sent a quick text to Sophia as the guys were jostling outside the sports complex. He typed, "Jn k… will call u soon," and sent in a hurry so as not to draw any attention. As John and Howard were walking to class John was right on cue and on the phone.

"Who are you calling?" enquired Howard.

"Sophia of course," said John. "Wish me luck," he added with a smile. "Hmm," he said, "Not answering. I'll send a text and call her later."

After physics class the two went their separate ways. Howard said, "See you at practice later," as he jogged off.

As soon as Howard got out of John's sight he called Sophia. She saw it was Howard and answered right away. Howard said that he couldn't even remember the name of the movie because his mind was scrambled with all the excitement. "I do remember it is about a woman boxer," he said, "Can you look it up?"

"I saw the trailer on that," Sophia said quickly. "The title is Million Dollar Baby. It will be perfect," she added with excitement. "You better tell all the players now so we're on the same page. Tell Coach Bell as well. Ok, got to go, John is calling me now."

Howard couldn't manage to get another word in the conversation but he didn't mind. He smiled contently. "I hope the movie is good or the guys will make me pay big time," he murmured to himself, the smile turning into a little chuckle.

The next 24 hours or so passed without incident. The entire basketball squad had more to think about than a movie date - the pain of Coach Bell's practice for one thing. "You guys have a full weekend off," yelled Coach, "We've got to make this practice worth thee days."

By the end of practice the players were exhausted. They all just shuffled straight back to the dorm for a good night's sleep. Night and day came and went. It was dark by 5:15pm on Friday when the teammates plus Coach and Sophia rendezvoused at the movie theatre.

"Ok, if everyone has a ticket let's go find some seats, and sit together," yelled Coach, as the players rushed down the corridor joking that if they could find seats and be quiet that maybe Coach wouldn't be able to find them. It was just good fun. It was true that Coach Bell was not "one of the guys" and that was his intention. "I'm the Coach, you're the players," he would remind them from time to time. Coach was very professional and the players respected him a lot. They knew that he had their best interest in mind all the time. They also knew that there was a time to be playful and it was ok to joke around at a movie although they also knew Coach would not stand for them crossing the "foolish line" or they would be "doing lines" at the next practice. Coach had taught the "men" in many and various ways that they had a responsibility to the university, the game of basketball, and themselves to be respectful of others. They executed their plan to sit together in just such a respectful fashion.

After they got their humorous message across, and Coach was seated behind the group, Skip turned and said, "Oh, Coach, we've saved a seat for you right in the middle," to which Coach countered, "Thank you all but I am perfectly comfortable enjoying my popcorn right here, as long as I'm not behind Skip because I wouldn't be able to see the movie." The guys chuckled and looked at Skip as if to say, "He got the last word," then settled down as Coach said, "The movie is about to start. Pay attention to the details."

Sophia sat on the outside edge of the group beside her brother John who sat by his team appointed big brother Howard. John wanted to sit beside Sophia to honour his original date. He did notice though that Howard was reaching over to share his popcorn and chitchat with her. John didn't know what to think about that. He was a bit jealous that Sophia was giving Howard so much attention. Perhaps his mentor was going sweet on his little sister. He didn't want to think about it and used the tactic of shushing them and reminding them to watch the movie.

Howard and Sophia's plan had worked like a charm thus far in more ways than one. It was a rather complicated and expensive way to get John to attend the movie so he could make it to his surprise birthday party. However, on the plus side, all the guys were raving at the movie. "Coach, you don't have many good ideas but this was a good one," joked Skip.

"I'll take that as a complement," Coach replied with a smile.

"Ok, now that we've settled that," said Howard, "Let's go for something to eat."

Skip opened his mouth as if to carry on joking with Coach. "Thank you for all your insightful comments," Howard said firmly to Skip before he could get a word out of his mouth.

"Hey man, I was just going to second your idea," he retorted, "I'm starving." In one voice the players told Skip to shut up and walk.

They were all a bit surprised when Sophia spoke over their noise say, "I know a great place to eat."

Howard immediately jumped to her support, "Well then, let's go," he said.

Howard and Sophia led the way. "Come on John," said Howard. "This is your neighborhood and we need your help to navigate," he joked.

John joined his sister and mentor. "Where are we going?" he asked Sophia.

"I thought we'd go to the Chinese restaurant right around the corner. They have an all you can eat buffet on Friday nights." Sophia was anxious, as she knew that John was only so-so when it came to Chinese food and was expecting him to disagree with her recommendation.

To her pleasant surprise John said, "Sounds perfect." He then added humorously, "And, we'll get very good value with this mob." Sophia felt relief for the first time in a week. If they could navigate the remaining fifty meters or so her special plan to honour her brother would pan out.

As they entered the restaurant John said, "What the heck. It is dark in here and no people. Are they closed?"

"It is Friday night, that's strange, very strange." Sophia gave John a little push through the door. "Let's go in and see," she said. As soon as they got through the doors the lights turned on and a rousing crowd jumped up with "Happy Birthday John!"

John was totally surprised and speechless. His Dad and Mom came up from their hiding place and gave him a great hug. Other guests were clapping and blowing horns and making a joyful racket. The light revealed all the decorations so tirelessly put up by family and friends including a large banner, "HAPPY 19th JOHN." The surprised birthday boy was totally at a loss for words and his many emotions were almost confusing. He dare not shed a tear in front of his teammates, he didn't have anything profound to say, and he had never experienced such a special occasion. "Imagine, all this for me," he thought and he did get a bit misty. Sophia motioned for the room to quiet and John spoke up simply saying, "Thank you everyone. I love you Mom and Dad and Sophia." He turned and looked at his teammates. With a pumped fist he jested, "I'll get you back for this." Then he turned to the guests. "Thank you all" was all John could get out.

John's Dad broke the silence. "Let us give thanks for this special night and this special son." After a brief prayer he announced, "Now then, let's enjoy this lovely buffet and get the celebrations started."

It was a wonderful evening. There was a ton of food. John found out that Mr. Leung, the owner of the restaurant, was a long time friend of his Dad and wanted to ensure all the guests were well fed. Sophia had organized lots of games and the conversations were flowing all night. It seemed the whole town showed up. All in all it was something very special.

The time came for the guests to disperse. To a person they departed with broad smiles and well wishes. John couldn't help but think about relationships and how important that they are for happiness. John stood with his family waving to the last departing guest. Love and gratitude were abundant.

Story - The Wandering

Dad walked back to thank Mr. Leung who motioned to Chef and staff to come and see the family off.

John thought about that night from time to time as the years went by. The thought of this special party brought comfort to him during the difficult times that would cross his path. Sometimes there were surreal moments too where he paused in awe at the thought of all the effort that had been put into making that party so special – and it was all for him. At these times he would give thanks for the love and support that he received from his family, friends and teammates – it was awesome.

By the time John was in his 3rd year at university those closest to him could sense struggle. It was also apparent in his results on the basketball court and in the classroom. Those closest to him and with his best interest at heart could see a good deal of slippage. John was still a starter on the basketball team but just hanging on. Talented younger players were working extremely hard to take his spot. By the end of the season his playing time was less than half that of the year before. Howard had long since graduated and John had not kept in touch. He didn't have a confidant now like Howard to share his fears and feelings with. He didn't even feel it possible to contact Howard as he landed a good job in Asia and thus was on the other side of the world. Coach was always there but John would not open up to him. Mom and Dad were available but then again there was no reason to bother them, John reasoned. "Things aren't that bad and it is normal to struggle," he thought. Sophia had moved half way across the country to attend university and she had her own life. "I'll catch up with Sophia this summer," John thought to himself and carried on.

It was an extremely tense meeting for John. He had decided over the summer to drop out of varsity basketball. He now had to tell Coach. John reasoned that he would spend more time on studies in his final year and get a higher graduating grade. That would help with a good job. "Coach would agree surely. And, Mom and Dad, will certainly support this decision," John thought using every sensible reason to convince himself that his decision was sound. John did not consult Sophia these days as he felt his little sister was grown up now and focusing on her own life. "There is no need to even bother her with such a trivial matter," he thought convincingly. "Anyway, it's only dropping basketball in order to do more studying." Still, John's feet were heavy that he shuffled through the door of Coach's office that day.

John was welcomed into the coach's office and invited to sit. "Coffee, tea, or soft drink," offered Coach.

"No, thanks," said John as he was anxious to get this over with. After both men sat down John raced through his sales pitch with all the reasons to support his decision to quit the team. Trying to relieve the tension and flatter Coach, John added that Coach Bell and his staff had recruited some excellent younger players and that the team wouldn't miss him with all that talent raring to make the starting five and claim their spot in university sports history. John looked down after he finished his pitch and then, after a few moments, eased his eyes up to look at Coach's reaction.

After a few seconds of silence Coach Bell responded to John. "John, do you know that I took a bit of a risk starting you as a freshman? I decided to take that risk because you were capable to fill the position and I also had every confidence that you would work very hard to justify my decision and keep the spot. And, I knew that you would be a good example to everyone on the team, especially the younger players. That decision and your response proved to be a good one. We even qualified for the national championship tournament two years ago." John smiled at the reminder of those great times but remained silent. John then tightened his lips and braced himself for a scolding. The Coach's words and expressions had brought a sense of pride and satisfaction to John. He was encouraged. Yet, at the same time an inkling of shame brought doubt into John's mind, bringing into question his reasoning for quitting. He thought Coach would surely recognize this, go on the offensive, and deliver the heavy guilt trip to cause him to change his mind.

Coach Bell paused and asked John a question, "John, is there any way that I can convince you to change your mind and stay with the team?"

John looked up with a querying expression. "You mean it is my choice?"

"Of course it is," said Coach, "It has always been your choice. I can only offer you to stay, which I am doing now - on the same terms of course."

"Yes, I know the terms Coach and they are fair," said John. "It is just that I feel this is the right decision for me. I can study more, get better grades…" John rambled as he started through the sales pitch again.

Coach didn't cut him off. He just smiled, let him finish, and then walked him to the door with an arm on John's shoulder. "Don't forget the good times we've had and everything you have learned," said the Coach as John opened the door.

"I wouldn't Coach," said John. "Believe me, I wouldn't," he added as the two men shook hands. John took a few steps and then turned to say thank you. His words stopped mid breath though as he noticed the door had closed quietly and he was alone in the corridor.

John stuck with his plan but the results were not exactly as he had expected. He graduated but without the distinction that he had set as his goal. "Social competition was just too great," he would jest to those that he had told of his plan for higher grades. "At least I have a good network and can leverage on it to get a good job," he would say, already adopting the lingo of business. John did secure a job in financial services selling bonds. It meant moving to New York but John was thrilled that he had a job that was bringing in good money. He also had ambitions to move up the corporate ladder and take on more responsibility – and with higher pay and bonuses.

John jumped into the job and lifestyle with vigor. The ability to focus energy for a time on what he set his mind to do was part of John's make up. He had shown this attribute as a youth by starting neighborhood business ventures. At one time he was delivering newspapers early every morning, running his lawn care business, and competing at basketball and baseball. He had lots of energy and didn't mind hard work. That was never a problem. But he did have a tendency to get distracted and have his energies diverted elsewhere. In any case, his mantra in New York was "Work hard and Play hard" – and he did!

The news of the collapse of Lehman Brothers hit John like a sledgehammer. He was nearing the end of his second year of trading bonds and was flying high. He, like so many others, could not believe that the 4th largest investment bank in America could fail and file for bankruptcy. In the whirlwind that followed John and thousands of others were downsized. While John had squandered most of his earnings, he had saved a little money so he felt that he wasn't desperate. However, after taking stock of his financial position, he knew that he needed to search for a job immediately and land one fairly soon.

Search he did and he did so with the usual vigor. But in a few weeks his confidence began to wane as the reality became clear that traders at his level might never get back in the game. John had exhausted all his contacts and used up his energy trying to find work. He still stuck to half of his mantra of "playing hard" reasoning that work would come soon and he would then have more than enough income to support his social life. It didn't take many months though until he was exhausted and discouraged to the point of not even looking for employment. But the landlord still demanded the rent for his apartment and other bills were draining his savings fast. John had been ignoring calls from his parents but when he saw a call on his phone's display from Sophia he gathered courage and answered it.

"How are you big brother?" opened Sophia in her usual exuberant tone.

"Fine," said John. "Well, maybe not so fine," he confessed as he shared with Sophia the disastrous effects of the subprime mortgage and bond fiasco. He bent Sophia's listening ear for almost an hour before realizing that he had monopolized the conversation venting his frustration.

"John, you have been through an unprecedented phase of banking history. If a portion of what we hear and read of this financial collapse is true then it looks like it might take months or years to recover. Can you hold out in New York by yourself until the industry recovers?" she asked.

John didn't know what to say. He had been so traumatized by the experience that he had lost perspective. It was true that his savings were becoming desperately low and he didn't want to borrow money. Banks would not loan him money in any case and that meant leaning on friends and family, which he had determined not to do. "I really don't know what to do Sophia. I just hope to find some work soon. I'm looking all over America, not just New York but everything is so depressed right now, it's really crazy." He was beginning to ramble again.

Sophia listened for a few minutes then opened her mouth at an opening, "Have you thought to contact Howard in Asia to see if there is any work there?"

John was stopped in his tracks by the suggestion. "Ah,

well, I never thought of that," he conceded. "I've lost track of Howard, do you have his contact?"

"Of course. I will text it to you," said Sophia. John's thoughts went to better times during his freshman year at university and the close relationship that he enjoyed with Sophia and Howard.

He changed the topic. "Sophia, I don't think that I thanked you enough for organizing that wonderful birthday party. I was such a bonehead wanting to go out to the pub instead of a movie with you. And all the work that you went through to get me to change my plans."

"What," said Sophia in surprise. "How did you know?" "Well," started John with some hesitation thinking now that he was betraying something told him in confidence, "Howard shared it before he left for Asia." He then added, "He also told me that I better take care of you or I'd have to answer to him!"

Sophia was silent.

"I thought that you knew that he had a crush on you," John volunteered. John could tell that he struck a cord with his sister. "Sophia, are you still there?"

Sophia collected herself and said, "John, I need to sign off for now but I want to ask a favor of you."

"Name it," said John. "Can you call Dad and seriously consider moving back home for some time until you can sort all this out?"

"Well, I..." "John," interrupted Sophia. "Yes, Sophia I promise," said John.

"Tonight," said Sophia with gentle firmness.

"Did any one tell you that you're an excellent salesperson Sophia," quipped John, "Yes, I'll call as soon as we hang up."

"Goodbye John, I love you," said Sophia with sincerity as she pushed the end call button.

John followed through and called his Mom and Dad.

They did not say much except to welcome him to come home. They offered travel money but John declined saying he was fine and just needed a place for a while to get back into the job market. "I need to sort out some things here with the landlord and such but then can I come," he asked.

His mother jumped in, "Sooner is better. We'll have your room made up here."

John did settle things that he needed to in New York and got the train home. On the way he realized that it was not only the trauma of losing a job that caused him to be depressed but also that a lot of "stuff and things" were confusing him. Why didn't life work out the way he intended? He was living the dream wasn't he? He had a good family upbringing, a good education, was a varsity athlete, and on and on. If anyone should make it then it should be him. John began asking a lot of searching questions and surprised even himself with the state he was in. For goodness sakes he was 25 years old with no job and seemingly no future. John was discouraged to say the least. He was also showing signs of sliding toward depression.

One day Dad said to John, "Hey John, guess who I saw yesterday? Coach Bell. He was asking about you."

"What did you say?" asked John with an emphatic tone of anxiety.

"Well, not much, only that you were back in town for a while. He said he'd love to have lunch with you."

John was silent and wrestling with his emotions. "Just what I need to have Coach say 'I told you so' and remind me that I'm a loser," thought John. But then he remembered that Coach had handled the 'quitting' the basketball team conversation with discretion and professionalism. "Yeh, I can trust him," thought John on proper reflection. I'll give him a call in the morning.

Coach Bell wasn't surprised to get the call from John but

was concerned with the tone of voice. He'd never known John to be as low as his voice indicated.

"Let's do lunch today then," Coach replied to John's question about getting together.

"Well, I..." John hesitated.

Coach added, "I know a good Chinese restaurant and we can have dim sum."

"I think I know that one too," replied John with a bit more energy in his voice.

"Shall we say 12:30 then," said Coach.

"See you then," said John.

John was already feeling a bit better. It was good to hear Coach's voice and it would be nice to have lunch out again. He and colleagues from New York ate out often and he began to think of times when he had money in his pocket. Coach, on the other hand, was preparing for hearing a painful story. He had been briefed by John's Dad and realized he would not be lunching with the happy-go-lucky freshman basketball player he knew. But it would be John, a good man in need of good conversation. Coach phoned Mr. Leung and asked him for a table in a quieter area of the restaurant.

Coach Bell was early and met John by the door. John commented that Coach looked exactly the same as when he played ball.

"You too," said Coach with a sly grin.

"Yah, except for an additional 75 pounds," quipped John. "I thought this was going to be an honest conversation," he added. Coach laughed and motioned John through the door.

The truth was that Coach did see a different person across the table. John was a good 75 to 100 pounds heavier than his playing days, and, he was obviously burdened by the pressures of life. But Coach Bell was an expert at seeing through all the junk and finding the person underneath. He'd been a coach for much of his professional life and his many accomplishments came as a result of him knowing people and how to get the best out of them. John hadn't considered any of that. He just knew it was easy to talk to Coach and that you felt better about yourself after doing so.

John thoroughly enjoyed their dim sum and conversation. Coach sipped his tea and listened attentively. He was genuinely pleased that John was looking so much better now. The burdens that he saw at the door had lifted momentarily, and the energy and enthusiasm of the old John was starting to emerge.

Coach easily discerned that John's hopes and aspirations for his "success" were deflated but he could see that positive attributes were still present in John. Coach Bell was feeling better about where John was at and felt it time to ask a piecing question.

"John, you intimated that you want a second chance. Why do you feel that you deserve a second chance?" John looked at Coach and was taken aback somewhat with the seriousness of the question. The lunch thus far had been about old times – good times.

"What do you mean?" John replied inquisitively.

Putting him at ease as only Coach could do, he leaned back and said, "Well, what would you do differently if you had a second chance?"

Feeling more at ease, John reflected and replied, "A lot. I would change a lot. Maybe everything." John then broke down and told Coach what a mess he had made with his life. He should have trained more and help the team win that championship they so coveted. "But I was lazy, pure and simple," he confessed. He continued to share that he should have gotten better grades to get his distinction award, do better at his job, get a promotion to management and so on. John laid out every failure in his eyes and places were he went wrong. Strangely, after sharing all this with Coach, John felt better.

He had confessed that his life was a mess but he felt clean and comforted in the presence of his coach.

"John, you are well on your way to a second chance," said Coach.

"What do you mean?" replied John lifting his head with an expression of surprise.

"Many people never get to the point of recognizing that something went wrong and that something is still wrong," he shared. "This is the point where the roads cross. Often people don't have a clue and just keep wandering. You know that you're at the crossroads and want the road that will give you that second chance. Does this sound about right?" Coach asked.

"More than about," John replied, "I know now that that is exactly where I am at but I am confused." John paused then astutely confessed, "I want to take the right road but don't even know how to recognize it."

"Well, we have some time before Mr. Leung will kick us out," Coach quipped, "Let's start with knowing where you are on the road by talking about Adultery."

"What?" said John with eyes bulging out and shocked looked on his face. "What are you talking about Coach?"

"I thought that would get your attention John," replied Coach, "Sometimes we need to be right in someone's face to get the job done."

"Right, like in basketball defense," said John. "You've got my attention Coach but I still don't get the question. Adultery, help me out here," John said with a genuine expression of enquiry.

"Ok, I know it is a bit heavy but it is critically important, and pretty straight forward too, so help me break it down," Coach began. "You must remember the chalk board in the team dressing room?"

"How could any of us forget," said John, "You always

wrote some gem of wisdom for us to apply to life and basketball."

"Right," said Coach, "And one of my favorites centered on two words; Wisdom and Understanding, do you remember?"

"Vaguely," said John, "Something about getting wisdom and understanding; and, do not forget my words or swerve from them. Yeh, that was it." John paused and looked at Coach. With a small chuckle he added, "The guys always joked that it meant always do what Coach tells you and you'll be wise."

"Well, perhaps I wasn't clear enough but I was hoping some of you might do a bit of research to connect the dots and figure out the puzzle of the words of wisdom," Coach countered. "Anyway, here is the full story now."

"Some of the pearls of wisdom that I wrote on the wall were from famous men or women like Mahatma Gandhi, Nelson Mandela, and Mother Teresa. Most however were from a single source, the book of Proverbs in the Bible. It is the best collection of wise sayings that I know of and I make it a habit to read the book once a year. I usually read it prior to each basketball season and made note of insights that I gained in order to pass on to the players. Anyway, there are a few chapters in the book of Proverbs that talk about adultery," said Coach.

"You've still got my attention," injected John with a look of genuine curiosity as Coach continued.

"It paints a picture of a woman whose lips drip honey and whose speech is smoother than oil. She dresses to invite the eyes of young men and comes out to talk to them explaining how wonderful it would be at her house with food, drink, and a bed with aromas of perfume, myrrh, aloes and cinnamon. She adds that her husband is away on a long business trip so they wouldn't be interrupted."

"Wow, I had no idea these kind of stories are in the Bible," said John still looking curiously at the Coach and wondering where he was going with this.

"Yeh, lots of good stuff in there. Anyway, don't get distracted by the gender and imagery as the writer could have easy explained the same truth personifying adultery as a man. Don't forget too that in that, in Proverbs, Wisdom is personified as a woman. But in any case here is where it applies to the crossroads where you are now standing."

Coach paused and observed John was anxious for his reply so he continued, "The full story paints the picture of a contrast of two lifestyles, one that is ruled by Compromise and the other by Wisdom. If you choose the "House of Wisdom" you partake in a life that introduces you to understanding, discipline, and blessing. And, contrary to what those in the "House of Compromise" say, living in wisdom is a great place to be. For example, one comment from Wisdom is that she is filled with delight day after day and rejoicing. Her house is a place of wholeness, generosity, and true love." Coach was studying John's reaction as he paused to give John a chance to respond.

"I guess I never really associated discipline and wisdom with fun," said John a little more subdued now. "What's happening in the other house," he asked.

Coach smiled and paused a moment. He could see that John was engaged in thought and anxious to learn. He then continued, "Well, first of all, your concept of discipline is exactly how everyone, including myself, has been fooled to think. We are led to believe that discipline translates to hard work for drudgery sake or taking a whipping from someone and such. Wisdom, however, explains discipline as an attitude that opens a person to receive instruction, teaching, and learning. It says something like 'Instruct a wise man and he will be wiser still' and compares that to the thinking of a naïve person who shuns discipline because it interferes with the fun he or she is having with friends."

Coach sat up in his chair. "Now, getting to your question," he said, "The book does explain what is happening in the other house that I called Compromise. The lifestyle there can be summed up in the phrase 'eating, drinking, and being merry.' They are having a good time, initially that is. But, as they go on, their character is compromised and their behavior deteriorates such that naivety turns to foolishness that progress to crime and heartache. Some may read it differently but I sense this is a gradual progression. One little step to get comfort from an attractive lady or man, or otherwise succumb to a host of other temptations, leads to a slippery slope toward other comforts and dependencies that eventually culminates in real misery."

John was sitting on his hands at this point and bowed his head slightly to look at his knees. "I guess that is where I am now," he murmured with a sense of failure and dejection.

Coach leaned forward and grabbed John's arm. John was now slumped forward in a heap of defeat. Coach then grabbed John's other arm and gently lifted him until his eyes rose. "John, believe me when I say that you are in a good place right now."

John was a little misty as he looked at Coach and queried, "What do you mean? I feel horrible."

"I can see that you do," said Coach as both men sat up. Mr. Leung had quietly placed a fresh pot of tea on the table and Coach poured some into John's cup. After sipping his tea, Coach broke the silence, "Remember the standing at the crossroads thing. I am convinced that you've decided to take the road to Wisdom and Understanding. Am I right in that assessment?," Coach asked.

John felt a wave of energy go through his body. His eyes

were bright like the John who tried out for that basketball team as a freshman. He was convinced by Coach's pep talk that his second chance was there for him to take. "You are right Coach," said John, "I'm going to take the option for a second chance and head down the road toward Wisdom and Understanding."

"Good for you John," replied Coach with a broad smile and pat on the shoulder, "I know you will find them."

John felt like he used to after a good workout. He was tired but stress free. He stretched his hands toward the ceiling, took a deep breath, and spoke, "I remember something else you wrote on the chalk board."

"Oh, yeh," replied Coach with eyebrows rising in anticipation.

John continued, "Take the first step in faith. You don't need to see the whole staircase, just take the first step."

"You were paying attention," said Coach with a voice of delight, "Dr. Martin Luther King, Jr. Right on John." Coach gave John a high five with the same vigor as if he had scored the game-winning basket.

Mr. Leung looked through the serving window that separated the kitchen from the dining area and saw the two men sipping on tea and laughing after each story of the good times they shared over basketball. Time was fleeting and John joked to Coach, "I can't believe we drank all that tea. My bladder says it is time to leave."

Coach burst out in laughter, patted John on the shoulder and said, "Good to see you still have that sense of humor. Hold on to it for the road ahead will still have a lot of potholes."

"Yeh, I can believe that but I still want to take that road toward Wisdom and Understanding," replied John with a tone of determination.

John headed for the washroom while Coach stopped at

the till to pay for lunch. "Looks like you had a good chat," said Mr. Leung.

"Indeed, we did Leung san. Thank you for arranging a quiet table and for all your hospitality," replied Coach.

"No problem Coach," said Mr. Leung with a smile, "My pleasure." John came round the corner and Coach met him at the door.

As they stepped outside Coach said, "John you could do with a project. How about helping me at rookie camp. And you might get a start at loosing that weight you added since your playing days."

"Thanks," said John, "I'll think about that and let you know. Can I call you about other things too?"

Coach knew that John would need an ear and some encouragement for his new journey. "Absolutely," he replied, then added, "Think about my offer John, but, in any case, a project is still a good idea."

As they shook hands and headed in opposite directions, Coach turned and said, "John, I'm sure that you know this but your sister has always wanted the best for you. She has always been in your corner."

"Don't I know it," said John. "I am blessed with such a sister."

"By the way, for information, I'm sure that you also know that the meaning of her name is wisdom. Maybe you can give a call to little 'w' while searching for big 'W'."

John nodded and waved goodbye. Then he stopped mid-stride and, in one of those eureka moments, said in a voice loud enough that could be heard in the distance that separated the two men, "Coach. A project. Why don't you just come out and say it?"

"Because it is so much fun hearing that penny drop when you finally get it," Coach quipped back.

"Ok, I do get it and I'm going to do it. It is Sophia's

birthday next month! Can you come to her party? Don't say anything though, it's going to be a surprise," John continued as Coach walked off chuckling all the way to his car.

John's mind was racing, "I'll invite Mom and Dad and Sophia's friends…" The list continued. A smile of complete satisfaction came to his face as he turned to go back to the restaurant and check available dates with Mr. Leung. "I'll call Howard too," he muttered to himself, "And I'll bet he'll not mind one bit to make that long flight to surprise Sophia on her special day."

The penny dropped again as he recalled the tone of Sophia's voice when she told him of Howard. "Hmm," thought John, "Indeed this is going to be a very special and most interesting project!"

Epilogue - In Search of Character
Compromise vs. Wisdom, John, and Character...

Character is one of those catch-all words that we use to project a mental image or communicate a concept. We intuitively understand that the word refers to one's personal qualities but we rarely have the urge to study its meaning. As we begin our search for character in a leader, it is worth taking a closer look at the meaning and etymology of the word "character."

Dictionaries help with succinct definitions; for example, "the mental and moral qualities distinctive to an individual; the distinctive nature of something; the quality of being individual, typically in an interesting or unusual way; and, a person's good reputation." (Oxford Dictionary)

The English word was borrowed from the old French "caractere," which arose from the Greek "kharakter," a word used for a stamping tool. The "stamp" or "chop" imagery suggests a heredity bias to one's character. Indeed, the idea of distinctiveness in one's character from birth is a commonly accepted understanding.

The mental and moral qualities that are stamped in one's being are however quite complex. They are subject to physical and spiritual forces that can and do influence and change them. Indeed, one's distinct character is intended to be dynamic and mature as it interacts with its environment.

The sciences of personality assessment and psychology help us to understand qualities that interact to shape a person's character. Leaders of social institutions are well advised to use knowledge of these sciences and others to help them assess and develop character.

Moreover, and this is key for current and aspiring leaders of social institutions to appreciate, there is a definite linkage of character and leadership development. Mature character is an attribute critical for sound, moral leadership. Those cast in a role of training leaders must recognize that they need to include character development in any plans to develop leadership.

John was born with character traits that defined him. We have to read between the lines to identify John's distinctive characteristics but it is clear that John has a great deal of talent and potential. Caring, loving parents who had the means to have him play competitive sports and receive a good education nurtured him and his character. John rode a wave of talent and achievement through childhood and adolescence. He was welcomed into an established and reputable university where he was distinguished as a varsity athlete in his first year. Presumably, he was achieving well enough at his studies too.

John was living the dream – or so he thought!

For, although John inherited talents that could be well used in leadership and was afforded the advantages to develop them, he hadn't noticed a couple of flaws that were seriously impeding his character development. John's ego was much too self-centred. It caused him to make a number of bad decisions and to form and maintain a view that he was entitled to prosperity and privilege. While it is common for infants to be the centre of attention and for children to be highly self-centred, it is critical in character maturation that one departs from that view of life and finds a healthy balance of self-hood and servant-hood.

The trait that is now commonly referred to as "entitlement" is dangerous to an organization when it is active in its leaders. Leaders who feel entitled to an unhealthy share will pillage the resources of an organization and harm it's reputation. It is sad to observe the damage that self-centred people in a position of leadership inflict on an organization because of an active trait of entitlement.

John confessed to Coach Bell that he was lazy. He always seemed to have lots of energy but closer observation would reveal that he didn't have the tenacity to finish difficult challenges. This lack of self-discipline prevented him from developing important leader qualities such as perseverance. Furthermore, he lacked the desire to manage and train his childish ego. His raw talent allowed him to acquire lots of awards for his silver platter but his character was immature and shallow even as he graduated from university and headed toward a responsible career in finance.

However, John's nature was essentially good. He was not only talented but had distinctively good characteristics. Moreover, his parents were diligent to instill a sound moral foundation and were, in themselves, good examples of Christian character. John's sister Sophia (wisdom) was also a positive influence on him. Indeed, John had opportunity from a young age to have his ego behave within healthy boundaries and to see to it that his character matured.

But he didn't!

Even with all the positive external influences, John would not recognize his rebellious nature. He chose to ignore it. This decision, whether conscious or unconscious, inhibited his character development. Thus, his character could not mature to the point where John could consistently exhibit strong moral behavior, or be trusted in positions of leadership.

Moreover, this immature character did not come to John's aid when he experienced life crashing in on him.

But an awakening came in John's life and he began the transition toward mature character. Coach Bell happened to be the right person who was at the right place at the right time to guide John to this transformational decision. Perhaps you have experienced the tutorage or mentoring of a wise coach or teacher and are thankful for their guidance. Perhaps there was a crisis in your life that caused you to call out to God for help – and He answered.

Fortunately for John, he came to that place where he could clearly see that his root problem was an undisciplined ego that caused him to be lazy, selfish, and rebellious. Enlightened now, John determined to follow the way that would lead him to the promises that his Creator intended for him.

Everyone's life story does not have a happy ending but we expect one for John. He has turned the corner and is determined to follow the path that seeks for wisdom and understanding. That way loves discipline and leads toward true knowledge. That way calls the wise to value humble nature that allows a person to develop mature, responsible, and reputable character.

Residing in the House of Compromise or the House of Wisdom, as Coach Bell put it, refers to the unseen forces that were affecting John. While John was shocked by the idea that he was involved in adultery, it got his attention and by the end of the conversation he experienced one of those "eureka" moments.

In fact, Coach had simply but effectively pointed out that John had closed eyes and ears to matters spiritual. This naivety opened John to the allures of comfort and temptation in its many shapes and forms. John's character was slowly but surely being compromised. He enjoyed all those things that stroked his ego yet was unaware it was even happening. Coach Bell knew John and had always been aware of his potential. He also knew exactly where the troubles in his life originated.

Because of his self-inflicted blindness, John had closed himself to real knowledge and wisdom. He was not remotely aware why the things he valued so much were all taken away. John had lost his position on the basketball team, did not achieve his academic goal, and got downsized from his job. His relationships weren't doing all that well either.

The tempter and a host of temptations, and the desires of his own highly self-centred ego, had been successful in causing John to "believe" that he "deserved" the silver platter. Rather that open his spirit to the gift of the Holy Spirit that cherishes such things as knowledge, wisdom, and discipline, John closed his mind and soul to such things. He was happy to "ride the wave" of his talents that allowed him to play on the varsity basketball team, get good grades, and take a high paying job that gave him money to enjoy life. John took for granted the advantages that where given to him by others and that allowed him to live an affluent life. He had the allusion that he was doing it all himself. The tempter's strategic plan to entice yet another person of affluence into the House of Compromise was working; until, that is, John opened his eyes and ears!

Circumstances came together such that Coach Bell could awaken John and see him start the walk on the "right path." Like all of us, John would continue to be tempted but at least now he had wisdom and understanding as comrades.

At this point… a reality caution…

Coach Bell could have been putting on a show but there are signs that he was a genuine leader of integrity. The wise sayings that he wrote on the chalkboard were backed by evidence that he actually believed them. He also practiced what he preached. In fact, Coach Bell's impact on his players was not due to his preaching at all but due to the consistent demonstration of righteous character. He was obviously well respected by his players and others for "right" reasons.

But beware…

In contrast to the genuine and integral character of Coach Bell, there are people skilled at putting on shows of good character but who are in fact bankrupt in the morals and beliefs that they profess. They would write wise sayings on the board then secretly practice the opposite. They reside in the House of Compromise. These are dangerous people as they are expert at "living in the lie." Put up your discerning antenna and take care not to be taken in by their appearance of propriety and respectability.

Back to John's story - from a Wanderer to a Searcher…

We can assume a happy ending to our first short story. John had transitioned from a wanderer to a searcher. His search led him to a place where a convergence of "right factors" got him on the "right path." He is positioned to understand and answer his "calling" in every sense (which we will explore more fully in the next story), and he finally got into a training program to get his character in shape for family, community, and corporate leadership. We don't expect John's journey to be easy. Quite to the contrary, the path he has chosen will have many trials, tribulations, and temptations. But we are confident that John will acquire the knowledge, skills, and accountability network to help him develop the first essential attribute of leadership; that of Character – mature, responsible, respectable Character.

Questions for Reflection and Follow-up Study

---

1. Recall President Abraham Lincoln's quote, "…To test a man's character, give him power." And, of course, this quote equally applies to women. Can you reflect and elaborate on his insight? In particular, what would you list as "power"? Are there other "temptations" that can test your character other than power? (E.g. affluence, pleasures)

2. Have you ever considered putting a value or price on character? Reflect on this and consider your answer.

3. Lincoln was surely referring to the fact that persons put in positions of leadership and authority will have power. And, one is subject to temptation to abuse that power. Can you think of any time that you abused your power or authority? Can you give examples of others abusing power? What was the cost of this abuse to your character?

4. Leaders in social sector institutions, and in fact all leaders, are subject to the temptation of accepting advantages. This temptation can appear every working day. For example, someone wants to influence your decision by buying you lunch or otherwise paying for entertainment, or, someone offers to pay a bill, put stamps on your personal mail, and/or give favours in various ways. Do you accept them? Is your character being compromised?

5. Read Psalm 139 verses 23 and 24. If you were to be searched, would any "offensive ways" be found in your character? How might you turn these to "ways everlasting?"

6. On honest reflection, are you residing in the House of Compromise or the House of Wisdom? (Recall the frog in the boiling water story. Consider if influences have lured you to gradually settle into the House of Compromise without realizing it.)

7. Have you contemplated residence in the House of Wisdom? Read Proverbs 3: 13 to 24 and consider if this is a place where you would like to permanently reside.

8. You have been put in charge of leadership development for management trainees for your organization. How would you go about incorporating character development into the program? Consider how you might: a) Test their character (remember Lincoln's quote) and b) Develop their character.

Prologue -
Courage to Answer a Call

Courage, the highest gift that scorns to bend
To mean devices for sordid end,
Courage – an independent spark from Heaven's bright throne,
By which the soul stands raised, triumphant, high, alone.
Courage, the mighty attribute of power above,
By which those great in war are great in love.
The spring of all brave acts are seated here,
As falsehoods draw their sordid birth from fear.

George Farquhar

But the LORD said to Samuel, "Do not consider his appearance or his height…The LORD does not look at the things man looks at. Man looks at the outward appearance, but the LORD looks at the heart." …

"So Samuel took the horn of oil and anointed David…and from that day on the Spirit of the LORD came upon David in power."

1 Samuel 16: 7 to 13

Author's note:
The setting for this story is in a country where English is not the native language, however, for ease of reading, I have used English names for the characters. Moreover, the "nicknames" for the people in the story point to the Christian heritage of the families. I reiterate that while inspired by actual events, the story is fictitious.

Story - Miracle

———•♦•———

May was the only child of David and Sarah. The family lived on a small farm on the outskirts of the city. Measured by the standards of established developed countries the property was quite small for a farm but it was sufficient for David and his family. The land was fertile and David was diligent in caring for it. In recent years, the paddies had given them many bountiful harvests of rice.

The high yields in the past two years however were attributed to the vision of a new leader of the province who had implemented a different system in crop production. Farmers were given incentives to increase their yields and they worked hard to do so. They had a quota to fill for government grain reserves and were allowed to sell any excess on the open market. There was already talk that this new system would become the model for the whole country.

David and Sarah felt fortunate to be part of this experimental new system and they worked very hard to ensure this commercial model of farming succeeded.

"May was born at a good time," David would often say to his wife when relaxing and sipping tea after dinner.

Sarah was silent but her facial expression affirmed her husband's hope for May. She poured her husband one last cup of tea and said, "Let's read some books with her and get her ready for bed."

The parents of David and of Sarah were not so confident to state that their children had been born at a good time. They were hopeful of course but considering what they had endured for close to two decades one could understand their reservations. There were numerous twists and turns in their lives as their country dealt with foreign occupation and its accompanying score of atrocities and heartaches. When the government had finally expelled the occupiers there was a struggle between two groups that had different visions for the country. David was born during this time of struggle with Sarah arriving just three years later. Their parents did however hope that their births would somehow signal better times for the country.

A new government was established. Rebuilding after such prolonged and severe conflicts was a challenge to say the least but Sarah and David's families pitched in with zeal and with every confidence for a better future. The promise of stability was in the air. May's grandfathers continued with their vocation of teaching at the university and worked hard to build a life for their families and do their part to contribute to the country's future.

David was a bright, lively child who loved to help his parents with chores around the house and engage in everything intellectual. David's father saw the love of learning in him and envisioned a time when his son would be employed in education, be it teaching, research, or administration. From an early age David recalled his father tutoring him at home. These sessions would routinely last late into the evening.

The first priority was always to complete work assigned by his schoolteachers. He could then enjoy other readings and projects prepared by his father. It came as no surprise that David finished top of his class year after year. In usual times David would have been able to apply to any university and be snapped up as a prime candidate. However, when David graduated from high school, times were not so usual. The promise of stability was short-lived as another major twist in the river of life and politics was on the horizon. David's father had to quietly use every contact he had made as a career academic and devoted citizen to manage his son's way into university.

It was the fall of 1962 when David's mother and father took him to the train station to depart for his first semester of university. Circumstances dictated that David study in a discipline that was not his first choice and at an institution a full three day train ride distant from his home. But he was fortunate to be attending university and a degree in finance and economics would place him in good stead for government service. David was determined not only to do well at his studies but also to like them. Due to the distance from his home, it was likely that his parents would not see him again until he graduated. The feeling of pride soon gave way to sadness and apprehension as David's mother and father waved goodbye and watched until the train was well beyond their sight.

David thrived in university life. He had lived in and around campuses all his life but that was not the same as the excitement he felt as a student. He loved everything about it. He was active in student affairs, engaged in university clubs, and, to his surprise, found all his studies interesting. The experience was opening his mind to the possibilities for him, his family, and the country. It was no picnic but David had never been deterred by hard work. His exam results for his first year were reflective of his effort and intellect. He ranked third out of the entire class of first year students. He worried that his parents would not be pleased, as he had always been first in high school. His eyes turned misty in relief as he read the letter signed by both his mother and father with the message that they couldn't be any prouder of him. He read though the letter a few times, cherishing every word and thought.

David's parents had a special box for storing the letters and had them filed chronologically. They had a practice of reading a couple of letters each night after dinner. Each time they did so they would pray for their son and contemplate a better future for their family. They felt together as a family in spirit at the evening meal.

Letter writing grew into an art for David with style and content of his letters showing distinct change as time progressed. In his first year at university David's letters were predictable. They would report grades and other academic progress, explain his involvement in other activities around campus, and generally brief his parents on how he spent his time. As David moved through his second year and on into his third year his parents noticed a change in his writing. There was progressively less space allocated to reporting on this and that, and more attention given to sharing his thoughts on various topics. He would share his views on economics and how renewed government thinking, policies, and practices could improve the country's economy and everyone's lives. Some letters would not mention his study areas at all but would speak to issues on life in general, including matters of faith, love, and family. Some letters even had poems in them. His parents would comment on how creative their son was becoming. Exchanging sheepish glances they would joke that he was now well prepared to send love letters to that special someone. They hoped and prayed that his choice for a wife would be Sarah, the daughter of their good friends. There was not any news forthcoming from either David or Sarah on that front and the parents decided not to broach the topic – for the time being at least.

David's father had noticed increasing tensions over the past year with university administrators. While he wasn't too involved in government, he sensed concern and frustration within the bureaucracy as well, particularly with regard to trying to recover from disastrously poor results from certain high profile initiatives. The economy had slightly recovered from a severe slump but the populace was still feeling the pinch. David's father did not want to worry his wife and speak of his concerns but it was clear that he was anxious. They had lived through some dreadful times and it was difficult to remain positive. "Hopefully this will just be a low ebb in the economic cycle," he said to his wife one evening during dinner. The very fact that David's father mentioned it indicated that things were bad and he was preparing his wife for rougher times still. "There are high school students coming on campus voicing their views loudly and stirring up trouble," he added, "I will write to David and advise him to stay clear of that group if they are on his campus." He pushed back from the table and move toward his desk. He glanced back at his wife and noticed her biting her lip to hold back tears. David's father halted his progress toward his desk and moved to give his wife a reassuring hug. "Don't worry. Everything will be alright," he whispered with all the confidence he could muster, "I'm probably overreacting but I wouldn't want David to inadvertently get into trouble. A little fatherly advice is timely, that's all." He then looked at his wife with an expression that communicated that this too would pass and everything will be fine. Then he sat down to write.

David received his father's letter and was startled. "I can't believe there is a similar group on father's campus," he thought, "I wonder if these groups are forming in other cities and campuses as well." David decided to send a letter straight back to his father with a brief message to the effect that although there was a group similar to the one he explained in his letter on campus, he had determined not to mix with them.

When David's father received his son's letter he breathed a sigh of relief. He too shot back a short note to David. "I was relieved to get your letter today. I am pleased that you chose not to mix with them. It is better to stay well away and just watch how matters develop. Don't be drawn into arguments. Looking forward to seeing you at graduation. Love, Dad."

It was a long journey for David's parents but they wouldn't let anything stand in their way to join their son for this special occasion. David was both excited to be graduating and yet a little anxious about the future. While he enjoyed his studies immensely, he wasn't sure how to find a job in his field. He knew that his father would support him in pursuing an academic career but David was more interested in commerce. In any case there were now disruptive groups in many cities that were forcefully advancing their vision for the country's economy - and their vision didn't align with David's. This was adding to his worries about securing a good job. His father gave him a squeeze on the shoulder and said, "Those are concerns for another day. Let's enjoy this special moment and then go home to consider the future." David smiled, took his advice, and enjoyed the weekend.

The countryside was a scene of enchantment on the long trip home and David was soaking in the changing landscape as if drawing a map in his mind. There were flat plains and delta flats as they headed west along the great river. These faded into rolling hills and mountainous areas. The various gorges and other features carved out by water and rain backed by majestic mountains caused David to marvel and fall in love with the land. Landscape gazing was broken from time to time as the family engaged in conversation and games. They thoroughly enjoyed the food that had been provided by friends they had stopped to visit along the way. As they recognized that the scenery was bringing them close to home the family of three became anxious for the journey to end.

David's father was a bit surprised to see Sarah's father at the station. They exchanged greetings and headed to their apartment near the campus. David's mother scurried to get the tea started and looked for some treats to entertain her husband's colleague. "No, thank you," said Solomon, "I can't stay but did want to have a word with Joseph about work." Solomon explained that a lot had happened in the few days that Joseph had been away.

"There is going to be a major review next week," he told Joseph, "I just wanted you to be mentally prepared for it. I don't know what to expect myself but do know that there are a few institutions on the list for review and leaders are not optimistic." Solomon turned to go then reversed to face Joseph. He whispered, "You should clean your house too. Stay safe my friend." He then hugged Joseph, turned and left.

That last comment and expression on Solomon's face caused Joseph to fully appreciate the gravity of the message. Joseph convinced Eve to burn all the letters they had exchanged with David over the past four years and also all the letters David had in his bags. It was heartbreaking but they wanted to ensure that there was no evidence of documents that may conflict with the ideology of the youthful authorities.

Institutional review was a term that administrators were using to send a signal to their staff and constituents that everything was normal. They hoped to reason with authorities and not be subject to some of the actions rumored to have taken place in other cities. That optimism was dashed, as the so-called review was more of an announcement of predetermined actions that institutions and people within them were required to do. There was little room for negotiation but knowing that his family would surely be labeled in a negative way, Joseph put forward a proposal that his son David be allowed to pursue studies in agriculture. One of the universities in the area had a program and he could enroll immediately. To his surprise the proposal was given conditional approval. The young authorities however added a condescending caveat that Joseph and Eve would also learn about agriculture – not at university but rather by experience from working on a farm. David too would need hands-on experience and a good record of working in the field before being considered as a candidate for studying agriculture. Joseph could see that the writing was on the wall. His work as a professor would come to a screeching halt but David at least had some hope of further study. When Joseph's so-called review was over he went home to explain the outcome to Eve – and to pack for travel to their new home.

The family was disheartened by the turn of events but when they considered their fate in light of what they had seen and heard of some others they determined not only to weather the storm but also to make the most of their circumstances. They convinced themselves to treat the disruption as an opportunity to grow mentally and spiritually. "This too will pass," was Joseph's wise counsel to his wife and son, "We want to use this experience to thrive and come out of it stronger."

The most difficult part for the family was the separation. David had just returned home after four years of study in another city. Now Joseph and Eve were heading to another region distant from David. The rationale muted by the authorities was that David needed to be away from his parent's influence so that he could be observed and evaluated if worthy of further study. David's father had not anticipated such a cruel response when he proposed the idea of allowing him to study but, as he learned later, many of the families were routinely separated in any case. When the time came to go their separate ways tears of heartache and deep sadness flowed. David maintained a brave presence and told his parents not to worry about him. The family huddled and prayed one last time. They had no idea when or if they would reunite.

The years that were to follow proved to be a major test of their resolve. For almost a decade David's parents labored in cooperative farming. David worked in the fields for six years before being granted permission to study agriculture at university. After his two-year program David was assigned as a resource person for a large cooperative. All the managers and workers were surprised at David's energy and knowledge. Yields improved within the first season. David's relational skills also helped him win the hearts of the workers. Within a year David had earned a place of respect and was considered an equal stakeholder in the operation. While the work was hard and the conditions harsh, David was satisfied in his work and in the place destiny had put him.

David's parents were faring less well. Joseph was an academic and he longed to get back into teaching. While he tried to make the best of the experience, as he had advised his son, Joseph did well just to survive the harsh conditions. At least he was with Eve and she was a strong person who supported and encouraged him. Together, and fortunately they were allowed to stay together, Joseph and Eve faced each new day with sufficient faith and confidence to be content.

As Joseph prophesized, the season of unusual circumstances they had found themselves in did eventually pass. A new leader emerged in government and brought in a renewed vision for the country. The impact on the heart of the people was immediate. There was a new sense of patriotism and love for neighbor. Understandably, the physical changes to improve the economy and stabilize society would take more time. Even so, the speed of transformation was quite amazing. There was widespread optimism that this would be a time of great opportunity.

Joseph and Eve were pleasantly surprised to discover that Sarah and David did end up exchanging those love letters that they had joked about years before. One of the blessings of the very difficult decade that the families had endured was the deepening love of David and Sarah. David decided that he would seek permission from parents to marry. Of course both couples were delighted. They did, however, as a matter of course and good fun, test David to ensure he loved Sarah and would make a good husband. While the future was still somewhat uncertain, this was a week for celebration.

David had used his time as laborer and student well, and he enjoyed the challenge of agriculture. He was still the same old David with an exuberant entrepreneurial spirit and he had a lot of great ideas for improving productivity. His background in economics and finance was also helpful. He very much felt part of the cooperative community. This sense of belonging was solidified even more when he and Sarah registered their marriage in the district.

Sarah and David decided that it was a reasonable time to start a family. As they were waiting for baby to arrive, David came home one day with news that a new provincial governor had been appointed and was causing quite a stir. A new system for agricultural development was being discussed. David of course was eager to participate. "These are positive signs," David told Sarah in a tone of sincere optimism. "I know that better times are ahead too," he added with eyes gleaming with hope, "A good future for our baby!"

The government moved quickly to implement the new

system. David couldn't believe his luck when he was told that he would be given some land to work plus some administrative duties for the district. It had been a long and winding road for both families but it now appeared that David could earn a good living and provide for his family – not only Sarah and their new baby but for the grandparents too. Some of the farmers had houses with space that was renovated and put on the market for rent. David found two such suites within walking distance from his house and negotiated an attractive lease arrangement. He and Sarah then invited their parents to take up residence near them. Their parents accepted with delight.

David and Sarah were proud of May. She was a healthy baby and it wasn't long before she was mobile. The pace of life picked up quickly for Sarah. David suggested that Sarah invite the grandmothers to come on rotation to help her care for May and otherwise help Sarah with chores. Sarah followed up on her husband's suggestion and each grandmother took three days on the weekly schedule. As it turned out, both grandma and grandpa would help with the childcare duty. The men filled in time playing with May and helping David with some of the lighter farming chores. May's grandfathers were still teachers at heart and they made a habit of finding books to read to her. May loved to read the books with her grandparents.

May was a good student and very responsible too. She had lots of energy and used it before and after school to help mommy and daddy with the chores on the farm and around the house. In school she was in the top quarter of her class academically and was quite a good athlete. The school did not have any sports teams but did have athletic days throughout the year where children could compete at running and other games. The school also had a basketball hoop attached to a pole in the playground. The pitch was often muddy as the pole was just dug into the ground, which became beaten down with all the activity. The netting on the hoop had long since worn out as well but none of that dampened the enthusiasm of the children as they ran, passed, and shot the ball with hopes of getting it through the hoop. May was quite a good shot so she was a popular choice when children were picking teams. Life was good for May and her family and they were blessed with good health, enough food and money, and loving relationships.

David had developed a reputation as a progressive thinker who could find his way through bureaucracy and administrative systems to get things done. His work in agriculture allowed him to more than adequately provide for his family. The economy was opening up too at a rapid pace. David's education, training, and tutorage from his parents had prepared him well for this season of commercial development. It was only a matter of time before David would be recruited for a bigger role in commerce.

May breezed through primary school and was a top student in her high school. David started to get calls to consider jobs in the corporate world. His education as an economist and experience as an agricultural entrepreneur had positioned him to work in the growing business sector. Banking was interesting to him and there was a major bank that was looking to recruit him. He accepted an invitation for an interview.

Sarah was happy for her husband. The only concerns she had involved the realities of change. They would have to leave their home in the country and move to the city. Three of May's grandparents had passed away and only Sarah's mother was alive now. She was living in the same suite David had leased so many years before. David told Sarah that if he got the job he would ensure they got a big enough apartment so that her mother could move in with them. Sarah also worried whether May would be able to cope with such a big move. She had lived her entire seventeen years on the farm. She would have to be separated from her friends. "Can we discuss all this as a family after dinner," Sarah asked David as she kissed him goodbye.

"Yes, sure, but they haven't offered the job yet," replied David.

"They will," said Sarah, "They will. But don't worry, I will keep it secret and let you break the news to May and Mom after dinner."

May was a little surprised to see her mother at her grandmother's place when she dropped by after school. May stayed after classes almost every day to participate in study clubs and sports, and had a habit of visiting her grandma before heading home for dinner. She ran and gave her mother and grandmother a hug. This was her natural habit since she was a toddler and being seventeen didn't change anything. She was the joy of her mother's life. "Grandma is having dinner with us tonight," announced Sarah, "You can help me walk her home."

On the way home Sarah asked her daughter, "Maybe you can sleep on the floor mat tonight so that Grandma can use your bed. It will be too late to bring her back after dinner."

May jumped with delight, hugged her grandmother and responded, "Of course you can use my bed, Grandma. We will have a wonderful sleepover."

It was time for dinner by the time the three women arrived home. Sarah went right to work getting ready to cook the food she had prepared earlier.

"Where is Dad?" shouted May over the noise of the kitchen.

"He is not yet back from his discussions with the people at the bank," replied Sarah.

May's face lit up. "That must mean that they like him," she said with eyes sparkling.

Sarah smiled. She was greatly relieved by her daughter's reaction. "Let's wait until your father comes home and we can discuss it then," she counseled, "But after dinner."

May and Sarah prepared the table when David walked in. He went straight over and gave his wife and daughter a big hug. "Well, what did they say Dad," blurted May.

"May, after dinner," said Sarah with a stern look while trying to hold back a smile. David glanced at his wife to see if her expression would agree with his suggestion for compromise as he said, "How about details after dinner?"

"All right then," said Sarah with an inquisitive smile. Then looking straight into David's eyes she asked, "Well, what did they say?"

"They want me to join them," replied David with a broad grin. Both May and Sarah jumped with excitement and David wrapped an arm around both his ladies and gave them a big squeeze. Grandma was sitting down. She didn't say anything but nodded with approval. David looked at the three women and said, "I smell something cooking. Let's get it on the table and enjoy another lovely dinner." He gave Sarah an affirming look and helped bring the food to the table.

The family gave thanks and started into the meal. Sarah kept pouring tea to keep the cups full. As David sensed that May and Sarah could no longer stand the suspense he took a big sip of tea and then shared details of the job offer. "Things will need to move along pretty quickly," he explained, "As they want me to start soon. However, we don't need to panic as we can make a plan and execute it in an orderly fashion."

"You are already talking like a bank executive," joked May. Everyone chuckled. David too was relieved that his daughter seemed to be taking this so well.

"You'll need to finish your final high school year at a new school in the city," explained David to May, "How do you feel about that?"

This comment caused May's adventurous spirit to pause as she thought about her friends. She looked down then lifted her head to look in her father's eyes. "I can do that," she said, "And don't worry. I can still keep in touch with my friends here and make new friends in the city. Don't worry, Father. I am very happy and excited!"

David did put together a plan that worked for everyone. Change often brings mixed emotions and this was evident during the process, particularly since the family, including Sarah's mother, had many friends that they needed to bid goodbye. David discovered that the city had a YMCA and he found a Church the family could attend. Both of these would help them develop another circle of friends and otherwise help them settle in a new place. David worked long hours but enjoyed his job immensely. May settled into her school, making friends and excelling at her studies.

Time seemed to pass quickly in all the activity of adjusting to a new residence. May was well into her final year of high school when David decided it was time for her to consider what university to attend and what subjects to study. There were good universities in the city and David had made some initial enquiries. The family, including Grandma, was finishing up dinner when David brought up the topic. After reporting on his survey of universities and courses and presenting some options David waited for May's reply. She was normally quick to respond but this time she was silent, couched in a methodical posture. David was patient. He knew that he had laid out a lot of information. He waited a while for her response then said, "What do you think May?"

May was confident in what she wanted to do after high school but was anxious about her father's reaction. She wanted him to approve of her choice but fearful that he would be disappointed. She said a silent prayer then replied, "I have thought about it a lot, Father."

"Yes," said David, his eyes now curious, "Please continue."

May then looked at her father and said, "I want to go to seminary and study for work in the Church. I have been thinking and praying about this for a few months and feel it is best for me."

David sat back in his chair. He looked at Sarah and her mother. They were silent but both their facial expressions communicated their desire that he support his daughter. David paused for a moment in thought then sat up and looked at his daughter. "I hadn't thought about that option," he said, "But yes, that will suit you very well and you will make an excellent pastor some day I'm sure." His words and tone were genuine and most affirming to May. He didn't bother to say more as May jumped from her seat to hug her father in appreciation. Both Sarah and her mother shed tears of joy as they saw how David was so quick to support May's calling to church work. "This is a new day in our family and country," concluded David, "Let us recall our many blessings and support our lovely daughter in her study and work." The family talked long into the night recalling stories of times past with all its trials, tribulations, and joyful times.

It was not a surprise that May excelled at her seminary studies. She was mature beyond her years and confident in her many abilities. Her high energy, vibrant personality, and strong desire to serve others were directed toward extracurricular activities, particularly projects to work with and help the less fortunate. Her leadership qualities were well noted by the faculty.

May was delighted that her grandmother was well enough to attend her graduation. On that glorious day there were many happy photos of the three generations. Sadly however, shortly after May's graduation, Grandma passed away.

At her grandmother's memorial service, May recalled

the wonderful times that she shared with her grandparents. "Those times were so precious," May shared, "My grandparents helped instill a wonderful faith in me and a sincere love for God and people. There is no doubt in my mind that the sacrifices and loving care of my parents and grandparents shaped who I am and contributed greatly to my calling to pastoral ministry."

Within a few years May had earned a reputation as a caring and insightful leader in the Church. The life of a pastor is very demanding and May's parents worried that the stress would be too much for her. Yet every time their paths crossed, May seemed as energetic and bright as she was as a child. She urged her parents not to worry as she loved her work and was in excellent health.

"It is a parent's job to worry," Sarah joked as she grasped May's arm and began walking toward the restaurant where they shared a meal each Sunday evening.

May laughed and said, "Yes, I am sure that you are right about that. Maybe I'll know the feeling some day."

"Is there something we should know?" piped David, now getting into the jovial spirit.

"Well, maybe," said May sheepishly. Sarah stopped, looking back and forth between her daughter and husband, with her jaw dropped in expectation. "Let's talk after dinner," said May with an aura of seriousness.

"Oh no you don't," quipped David, "That never worked before when I had news. Don't keep us in suspense." Sarah's eyes were sparkling with curious anticipation by now.

"All right," said May, "It is just that I met someone and he is pretty special to me." Sarah looked intensely at her daughter, "And does he feel the same?"

"Yes, I believe so," confided May.

"Then I better meet with this young man," injected David in a responsible fatherly fashion.

May's spontaneous nature took over as she blurted, "How about I call him and invite him to join us for dinner?"

Sarah was not quite ready for such an impromptu response. "Well," she said timidly as she glanced at David, "I'm not sure if we're prepared." Her body language indicated deference to David's decision.

David looked at his wife and gave a lighthearted response, "This is the world we live in now Sarah. Everything is moving at top speed." David then looked at his daughter and said, "Why not. Give your friend a call." He wrapped his arm around Sarah's shoulder and gave a loving squeeze. He then turned to May and asked, "Oh, what is this friend's name?"

"Chi Tim," she answered, "But all his friends call him Tim."

"Tim it is then," said David.

Tim hit it off with the family right away. He was respectful and quietly confident with a good sense of humour. Time passed quickly in cordial talk and wide ranging conversation. The restaurant was about to close as the four departed.

David and Sarah were both satisfied in their spirit that Tim was a good man. He and May were obviously in love and the parents were hopeful that Tim would be a good husband for May. Over breakfast the next day David mentioned to his wife that they should be patient and just wait and see if Tim and May's relationship matured. "I want my daughter to be as happy as I have been," he whispered to Sarah as he hugged her before going out the door for work.

Some months later David got a phone call from Tim and after cordialities he said, "I wonder if I can come over early tonight before dinner. There is something important that I'd like to discuss with you."

David told Sarah about the phone call. She was expectedly excited anticipating the important matter Tim wanted to discuss was about marriage. Tim did arrive early for dinner as planned and was invited into the sitting room for tea. After a sip of tea, a nervous Tim got right to the point and went through the formalities of asking David for permission to marry May. Sarah was listening in from the adjacent room. David stood and called to his wife to join them. After a protocol of questions similar to those asked of David when he sought permission from Sarah's father to marry her, David gave Tim his blessing. Sarah was jubilant and gave Tim a hug.

"Don't tell May at dinner," Tim requested, "I want to surprise her later tonight with my proposal."

Sarah could hardly contain her excitement during dinner but did a good job of not disclosing the secret. After she served desert, Sarah suggested an early evening citing that David had a meeting the next morning. David took the cue and masterfully called the evening to a close.

May did accept Tim's proposal and they worked toward setting a date that was both auspicious and convenient for family and the logistics of the wedding celebration. While May, Tim, and both families favored a simple wedding they couldn't escape the facts that May was the pastor at a Church of significant size and David now had a senior position in the bank. Also, the fact that Tim had so many relatives and friends in the city made for a rather large wedding invitation list and banquet.

When the banquet festivities had ended and the guests had departed, the parents of the bride and groom reminisced of times gone by. With the noise of staff cleaning the banquet hall as background, the two parent-couples shared numerous stories of the children growing up evoking laughter, smiles of pride, and even tears. "The river of life has had many twists and turns for all of us," David said reflectively, "Let's pray that the river runs straight with many trees on its banks for our grandchildren."

May and Tim saw no reason why they should delay starting a family. As their first wedding anniversary approached May was heavy with child. A few months later May delivered a healthy baby boy. They decided to name him Isaac.

"He is such a happy baby," said May, "And I know he will bring much joy and laughter to our house."

Tim concurred with his pastor wife that Isaac would be a fine name for their baby. Although it is every parent's hope, May's prophetic statement of the boy bringing laughter and joy to their house was very true for their family. He was an easy child in that he slept well at night and adhered to his nap times. When awake he was active and curious with a pleasant temperament. Life was good for May and Tim and their baby boy Isaac.

May was fortunate to have a mother that lived less than twenty minutes walk from her home and who loved to help with the day care. Caring for Isaac filled Sarah's days with happiness and allowed both May and Tim to give carefree attention to their work. As Isaac graduated from crawling to toddling, Sarah could take him to more play areas where he could wear off some of his high energy. One place they visited most mornings was the church where May was pastor. This allowed Isaac to play with his mother for a few minutes while Sarah relaxed. When her brief reprieve was over, Sarah would watch over Isaac as he played outside. When the weather was harsh Sarah would set up a play area for the toddler inside the church building. Whenever May's schedule would allow, she would have lunch with her mother and son. After lunch Sarah would herd Isaac home for his afternoon nap.

One day there was a tragic break to that routine. Isaac had a snack with his mother as usual while Grandma relaxed for a few minutes. Two years old now, Isaac was beyond toddling and running Grandma off her feet. He was a good and obedient boy but active. He also liked to climb. Isaac escaped from the view of both his mother and grandmother and headed for the outdoor exit staircase. It was an open staircase located on the second level of the church building that led to an area outside where Sarah would take him to play after snack. Isaac was familiar with the staircase and was mobile enough to manage walking down the stairs one step at a time as he held on to the rail. This morning however he tried something new. He raced to the staircase and climbed up on the railing. He was laughing with excitement when suddenly he lost his balance and fell. Sarah's heart dropped as she heard the laughter change to a thump then an injured cry. Sarah screamed for help and ran to where the toddler lay on the ground. By the time she got there Isaac had stopped crying. For an instant she was relieved then realized that the boy's eyes were closed and she screamed in agony.

In response to the scream, May and other church staff ran to the scene. "Oh God," May prayed, "My baby. Please save my baby."

One of the staff had rushed to get the car. There was no time to waste. The baby was breathing but they needed to get him to the hospital. Even calling an ambulance would take too much time. May gathered Isaac in her arms and got into the back seat of the car. The driver took them directly to emergency where the hospital staff rushed to May's aid. When Sarah arrived with other church staff they saw May on her knees weeping. They all joined in a huddle on their knees with tears flowing.

One of the church staff had called Tim and David and they too rushed to the hospital. Tim got there first as his place of work was much closer than David's. By the time David arrived almost two hours later he had no sooner given a consoling hug to May, Sarah, and Tim than the surgeon came through the doors. He explained that Isaac had no broken bones and all his vital signs were stable but that he had sustained a severe head injury. He had done minor surgery to relieve pressure in the brain due to swelling and they were monitoring him closely in ICU. The doctor further explained that the baby was in a coma but that he was responding well to treatment so he was hopeful the boy would recover.

Six weeks passed and Isaac was still in ICU. The stress was taking its toll on every member of the family. A good night's sleep was non-existent and, regardless of ones faith, the worry over the well being of their baby was affecting every aspect of life. May was in her study at the church when the call came from the doctor. "Isaac has wakened," he said with a tone of cautious optimism, "Can you come here as soon as possible?"

May could barely control her glee. She called Tim and asked him to call the rest of the family while she went to the hospital right away. May was in the ICU talking to Isaac when the other family members arrived at the waiting room. Tim was allowed to go in and join May but the grandparents had to wait outside. It seemed like a week to David and Sarah but it was less than an hour when Tim and May emerged to report on Isaac. May's eyes were full of tears. Tim was the one to speak. "He is out of the coma and aware of who we are," he started. Both parent-couples were silent in anticipation of his next words. "He only said two words; Mama and Papa. We were greatly relieved and encouraged by that but it is obvious that he will need a good deal more time to recover." Trying to keep a brave appearance, Tim collected himself and added, "The doctor said it will be good for us to be here and talk to him for 15 to 20 minutes each time he awakes but not more so as not to strain him. May and I will stay here."

As the days passed, the grandparents also took shifts talking and reading to Isaac. On the doctor's recommendation, Sarah took more shifts than the others because Isaac was more likely to respond to her. It took a few months but the time came when Isaac was able to leave the hospital.

The news was not as bright, however, as everyone had hoped and prayed for. Isaac was walking and functioning but the injury to the brain had severely impacted both his mental and physical development. He was three years old now and barely able to speak a word. His movement was spastic and he was obviously delayed in every aspect of his development. May would have normally been looking to register him in Kindergarten but now she was facing the reality that special schools may be all he could handle. Isaac was still a happy, loving child able to evoke laughter. But there was also a sense of sadness that this tragic accident had taken Isaac's full potential away.

After some months the family had adjusted to Isaac's condition and had accepted the reality of their new lifestyle, radically changed as it was because of Isaac's accident. May and Tim had long discussed and now decided to seek permission to have a second child, which required approval from the regional authorities. May and Tim would not have normally received any consideration at all except for reasons associated with Isaac's handicap. But this too was not all that simple. The regional authorities needed a lot of documentation to justify that Isaac was permanently disabled. An application was submitted and this triggered an investigation by the national authorities.

May and Tim were pleasantly surprised that the officers sent to investigate and report on Isaac's case were very cordial. They even felt them caring and compassionate. However, the officers had made it crystal clear that they were duty bound to be thorough and that their report would be comprehensive and based on objective data, not emotion. May and Tim felt comfortable with that approach although they found out it meant answering hundreds of questions, filling out forms, and briefing the medical professionals. The process took its toll on the family's emotions. "It was like being on an emotional roller coaster," Tim would explain to friends later, "You thought the application process was complete then all of a sudden more questions and a few weeks pass." Finally, a thoroughly documented report was submitted to the authorities.

They had just sat down for dinner when Tim and May heard a knock on the door. Tim slid his chair back and went to the door. To his surprise there were two county officials standing there with papers in their hand. "May," yelled Tim, "Set out two places for our guests."

Tim was sincere in his spontaneous invitation to dinner but the head official politely turned him down. "No, thank you," he said, "We cannot stay and we could have called you tomorrow but your house is near my regular route home and I thought you would want to know as soon as possible."

By this time May was at the door and pulling them into the living room. "It's about our application?" she said.

"Yes," said the head official, "It has been approved."

"Here is the paperwork," added the junior officer as she handed an envelope to Tim.

May and Tim thanked them profusely. Tim asked the officials again to join them for dinner. The officials knew it was a time that needed to be left for the family.

"We'll make it a lunch someday in lieu of dinner," the head officer said to Tim as he pushed the junior toward the door.

"We are happy for you," said both officers as they waved goodbye.

Years later Tim and May would share with their closest friends that they had mixed feelings about their decision to submit an application. Nagging them through the entire process where questions of motivation. Did their action suggest lack of faith in their God to heal Isaac? Would it indicate that they didn't love and appreciate their handicapped child? Would people think they were dissatisfied with their fate?

"Such questions were constant companions to both of us," explained May one night with a circle of friends, "And they caused us to doubt many things. We were content with our fate - sad but content. And we certainly didn't love Isaac less because of his handicaps – indeed, perhaps we loved him more. He is truly a blessing to us."

Tim would look at May and gently interject, "But these questions eventually disappeared, especially when our baby girl Elisha was born. We realized somehow that God approved all this. We have another child to love just as much as we do Isaac. It is really a double blessing," he would conclude with a broad smile.

Isaac was only seven weeks away from his fifth birthday when baby sister was born. Isaac was intrigued with his baby sister. He loved to lie on the floor and play with her. Sometimes he could keep her attention for 30 minutes or more. This was a good break for Sarah who looked after both children now. May and Tim knew that Sarah was guilt ridden by Isaac's accident but they also realized that it was not her fault. Sarah was an excellent caregiver and the children loved her very much. When the guilt would surface and start weighing on Sarah it seemed that Isaac would somehow sense it and give his grandma a cuddle. He was a sensitive boy with many lovable qualities.

One evening when May returned home for dinner Sarah said, "Oh, Mommy, Elisha has something to show you." Sarah stood Elisha on her feet and she immediately took a few steps toward Mommy who had already taken the cue and was waiting on her knees with arms outstretched. As Elisha reached May she laughed with the joy of achievement. May, Sarah, and Isaac celebrated.

Tim walked through the door and smiled at the commotion, "What's all the excitement?"

"It's official," said May, "Elisha is now a toddler!" Tim let out a celebrative hoot and walked quickly over to give Elisha a hug. Isaac came over too to get his hug.

As Sarah was putting on her jacket to leave she said to May, "Honey, I have been afraid to mention this to you but I think Isaac is improving quite a lot. He has been talking to me, sometimes nonstop, and his movement seems normal at times." May gasped and her eyes filled with tears. Since that terrible day May had been on her knees multiple times each day praying for her Isaac. She had always hoped for healing. Now her mother's words evoked pent up emotion. She put her head on Sarah's shoulder. "Thank you for telling me Mommy," said May, "Let's continue to pray for healing."

Tim noticed May had been weeping. He stopped playing with the children, gave her a hug and asked, "Are you alright?"

"Yes, fine," she responded, "It's just all the pressures. Not to worry." She patted him on the shoulders and put the food that her mother had prepared on the table.

"We must have the best baby sitter in the world," joked Tim as they settled for dinner, "She not only does a great job with the children but is a great cook."

"Yes, Grandma makes yummy food," said Isaac with a wide smile. Everyone laughed then gave thanks and enjoyed dinner.

As May was cleaning up after dinner she determined to methodically log Isaac's progress. After the children were tucked in, May talked with Tim, sharing what her mother had told her, and about the log she decided to keep.

"I've noticed some improvement too," Tim said to his wife, "I support what you are planning. I will help too, whatever you want me to do." The couple retired that evening with renewed hope.

May, Tim, and Sarah were not the only ones to see Isaac improving. In the weeks that followed May's determination to quietly log Isaac's progress, she received dozens of comments from parishioners concerning their observation of how well he was communicating, running, and playing with other children. May took every opportunity to thank them for their care and prayer. Indeed, on the joyous occasion of Isaac's sixth birthday party, he looked every bit as normal as his friends of similar age. This dramatic improvement in Isaac's condition was now being noticed by virtually everyone who knew Tim and May and of Isaac's accident. May continued with her logging of the various cognitive and physical measurements that the medical team had used during their assessment of Isaac's development in the months following his accident. She also brought in a friend to help who was an expert in child development. One day her friend declared, "I don't have the authority to claim Isaac mentally and physically fit, but, as far as I can determine, he is within normal range on all the assessment measures for his age."

Imagine the joy in the family. They all knew in their hearts that it was a miracle of grace, somehow granted by God. And yet, this miracle now presented some very real practical problems. The assessment by the medical professionals had officially classified Isaac as "mentally handicapped" and thus he was not allowed to enroll in school. To have such a decision reversed would surely be a rigorous and tedious process. It would be risky as well because Tim and May had received permission for having a second child, Elisha, wholly on the evidence of Isaac's handicapped condition. Tim and May would surely come under the microscope.

It was a delicate matter but there was no question that Tim and May would make their decision in Isaac's best interest, not their own. The application was submitted to have Isaac reassessed and reclassified as normal and, as anticipated, it did indeed cause Tim and May to come under the microscope of officialdom. The process was long, rigorous, and stressful. Isaac was cheerful for the most part and in fact seemed to enjoy all the attention that he was getting. But the attention aimed toward the parents was not so enjoyable. Investigators were looking for evidence to build a case for fraud and no stone was being left unturned. The same scrutiny that came into play to classify Isaac as mentally handicapped was reinvigorated but now it was even more vigilant.

Tim and May were shaken by the intensity of the interrogation. One evening, after the children were in bed, May tearfully suggested to Tim that perhaps they consider a different route. "Maybe we should try to get permission to emigrate or have Isaac enroll in a private school."

With May's head buried on his shoulder Tim responded, "I fully understand what you are saying. My day was pretty stressful too. My boss told me this morning that he wanted to support me but I'm missing too much time at work due to the need to be available at a moments notice to attend another interview. I was pulled out of an important meeting in the morning. After I returned late in the afternoon I met with my boss. He didn't say he would fire me but I could tell that he was coming under pressure too."

The couple consoled each other then knelt in prayer. Afterwards they went to the bedroom of their two children who were fast asleep. They kissed them on the forehead and retreated.

Tim smiled at May and with a renewed spirit said, "This will make for an exciting story for our children someday."

May smiled and said, "I agree. Let's continue. This too shall pass and our Isaac will go to school right here with his sister."

The weeks did pass and while the scrutiny was ever present it did fade in its intensity over time. Finally the day came when Tim and May received an official certificate that declared Isaac normal. He could now be registered for school.

Isaac would be a full year behind his peer group but that was acceptable to Tim and May. "The school Principal would surely promote him in the course of time as the teachers recognized his abilities," the couple reasoned. In any case it was a time to celebrate.

Some weeks later Tim and May were at a restaurant having lunch. The two officials from the county office who oversaw Isaac's case entered and caught Tim's eye. He immediately stood and went to greet them. "Remember that lunch you suggested in lieu of having dinner with us," Tim joyously said. "Come join us." The two officers accepted and sat to join them. Tim motioned to the waiter and places were set.

Toward the end of the meal the senior official congratulated them and explained that the rigorous assessment and collection of medical information following Isaac's accident proved crucial for the original decision to be reversed. "At the end of the day, the proof of Isaac's brain damage and developmental delay was so conclusive and so meticulously complied that the officials from the capital could not ignore it," he stated, "And certainly they could not disprove it. I know it was stressful for you at the time but that thorough process proved essential in this case."

Tim and May were beaming. With a broad smile and his arm around his wife's shoulder Tim asked, "We haven't received a copy of the official report yet, only the certificate verifying Isaac's reclassification as normal. Is there a reason given in the report for them to reverse the decision?"

The question caused the two officials to pause and look at each other. They were both smiling broadly. The senior official looked at Tim and May then broke the silence by stating, "Yes indeed. And you will get a copy soon."

May could not contain herself and leaned forward to seek a definitive answer. "Well, are you going to keep us in suspense or tell us," she said.

"Sure, sure," said the official, "As I said, you will get official notice soon but they simply concluded that it was **a miracle**."

Tim and May looked at each other then the officials. With teary eyes May squeezed Tim's hand and responded for both of them, "A miracle, yes indeed it is a miracle. Thanks to our God for giving back our Isaac."

Tears welled up in the eyes of the officials as they witnessed the depth of joy gushing from May and Tim. Hugging her husband and looking at her guests as they prepared to leave, May suddenly relaxed her right arm from its grip on Tim and pointed to the heavens. She then quoted from Psalm 109; **"Let them know that it is your hand, that you, O LORD, have done it."**

Epilogue –
In Search of Courage and Calling

We will now examine two more essential attributes of social sector leaders, those of courage and calling. We can also consider how character links to "true courage," which allows one to accept their "callings" in life and vocation.

Miracle, May & Family, Courage, and Calling...

As I started to write about a relatively recent incident involving a miraculous healing of a child, I discovered that there were many examples of courage and calling in the three generations that appear. In fact, the story that you read was inspired by events and experiences of a number of families that I wove into one.

However, I want to reiterate that I was generous in embellishing details of these fictitious families for reasons intrinsic to the leadership lessons that are contained therein.

Courage and Calling...

I felt it important to bookend May's story of call to pastoral ministry and the courage that she possessed to accept that calling, between the stories of her parents and grandparents, and a miracle. Indeed, as I started to write, I was drawn to the importance of family in child rearing and in nurturing minds and spirits capable of recognizing a "Call."

But, what is meant by a *"Call or Calling"*?

Gordon T. Smith writes in his book "Courage and Calling – Embracing Your God Given Potential" that the word calling can be considered in three different senses or expressed vocationally in three different ways; a general call to Christianity, a specific call to one's vocation, and an immediate call to daily integrity. Smith also asserts that calling is a demonstration of the love of God and the initiative of God. Inspired by the excellent content in Smith's book, I jotted the following personal notes on the three senses or contexts of a call in one's life:

1. We are called to be recipients of God's love and salvation. Right relationship can be restored, or at least revived, if we accept this call, and in turn we receive the ability to truly love God and love our neighbours;
2. We are called to find meaning in life and vocation (which may be quite different from career) through the first calling; and,
3. We are called to live in the moment with integrity.

Smith makes mention of a commonly held view that a call to vocation is reserved for persons engaged in full-time church work but he explains why that view is not supported biblically. He masterfully presents a case backed by sound theology that this supposition is wrong. Indeed, people are called to vocation outside the institution of the church.

Dr. Smith devotes a full chapter (7) in the 2nd edition of his book to elaborate on places of vocational calling. He categorizes these places as: Business and Commerce, the Arts, Education, and Religious Leadership. Within each of these four broad categories are a host of disciplines. Each and every

Epilogue – In Search of Courage and Calling

one of these disciplines can be God's gift and expression of His grace should one be true to his or her calling.

I fully embrace Smith's case that one can be called to vocation outside the employ of a church. However, I wrote of May's calling to pastoral ministry because that is actually the vocation that she felt called to and chose to pursue.

May was born and raised at a time when young people in her country could look to the future, hope for a vocation that provided both means and meaning, and prepare for that work in school. We easily accept in the story that May was called to her work in the church. She clearly articulated that she felt God lead her to a decision to study at seminary and there were regular signposts along the way affirming her call.

The tragic accident tested the faith of May and Tim. With her beloved Isaac lying in a coma, May must have had serious doubt and questions as to whether she interpreted her calling correctly. Surely God would not have called her to pastoral ministry and have this happen to her baby right at her own church!

A call to vocation is subject to physical and spiritual attack and there will be times of doubt. Prepare for that eventuality.

Isaac's healing was a miracle. It was further affirmation of May's calling but it was much more than that. May and Tim had already accepted Isaac's condition after his accident and were at peace within themselves. May had overcome her doubts and did not need further affirmation of her calling. So why did God order Isaac to be healed? We can't answer that question with any degree of knowledge. We can only follow the response of May and Tim and offer thanksgiving and praise for "His Grace."

When writing the story I did wonder if the reader would unduly identify to May's calling due to the conditioned bias that I refer to above; i.e. that "calling" is reserved for persons engaged in full-time church work. This may have caused readers to overlook the calling of other characters in the story.

Allow me now to assure you that both David and Sarah, and indeed their parents, had a call to faith, vocation, and daily integrity – and they answered it.

Again, Smith helps us understand the truth in my last statement. Recall that there are three senses of calling that demand differing expressions. We see these three senses played out in the lives of David and Sarah and their parents.

My respect and appreciation for the characters of all three generations grew, as I better understood the context of their lives. Indeed, the courage they exhibited to respond to God's call to life and vocation was incredible, particularly given their circumstance in history. The grandfathers were privileged to receive a good education and otherwise engage in intellectual pursuits. They were perfectly positioned to make significant contributions to family and society. I am not sure if they would have viewed "calling" as I describe it but none-the-less they would have had been of the minority that accepted the call to become a Christian. I know too that the men would have pursued their work at the university both as a means to support their family and as a meaningful way to serve society. The wives would have been supportive of their husbands and also would have been ahead of their time in advocating for the advancement of women and their rightful role in family and society. The personal character and integrity that they needed to face the unusual trials in their history would have been real and significant.

Yes, May's grandparents were called to a faith practiced by a small minority, they were called to train the intellect of young people, and they were called to live a life of integrity at home and in the marketplace that exemplified the righteousness of their faith.

The horrendous social and political realities that disrupted their life and intended to dash their dreams would demand "true courage" for them to stay true to their calling.

Epilogue – In Search of Courage and Calling

Both Sarah and David inherited the courage and conviction of their parents. They were born at a time when conflict was prevailing but when hope for socio-political security was high. That hope came to pass and for a brief time everyone was engaged in nation building. But the hopes and dreams that David's parents had for him began to unravel. The families found themselves in circumstances that they could not control. The river was flowing quickly and they would do well just to steer their family boat toward safe waters.

There are clues in the story that lead us to an understanding of the third expression of calling outlined above – that of living each moment of each day with integrity. None of the characters in the story could have successfully steered the ship through turbulent waters without understanding their call to be people of integrity. It was this intrinsic understanding of being "called people" that positioned three generations for family and community leadership.

Recall the wise counsel that David's father gave when they were about to be separated and sent for reeducation. First he gives an expression, "This too shall pass." There is a dual meaning to this phrase from ancient folklore; one, that during times when one is in the depth of affliction they can be comforted by the fact that it will surely pass; and also, when one is puffed up with pride, recalling this phrase serves as a reminder for them to return to a humble centre where wisdom resides. While not a quote from the Bible, this phrase is also commonly linked to the Apostle Paul's teaching in 2 Corinthians 4:17-18 where he presents troubles as transient yet, while troubles are active, they serve to build faith in the eternal glory promised to believers in Christ.

This understanding would reinforce the family's hope that the affliction they were about to experience would pass and they would actually benefit spiritually from it.

Secondly, Joseph (David's father) advises his son and wife

to use the experience to thrive and come out stronger. That was the attitude of one called to teach. Joseph was called to be a teacher and an encourager. He remained true to his calling and beliefs despite difficult circumstances.

Family members could not have envisioned that this trying time would stretch toward ten years. Great courage would be required to persevere and thrive through those severe times. Let's look closer at this third essential attribute of social sector leaders.

Courage is counted as one of the four cardinal or pivotal virtues of western society (the other three in ancient Greek being prudence, justice, and temperance; although, we add more today).

Maya Angelou adds, "Courage is the most important of the virtues, because without courage you can't practice any other virtue consistently. You can practice any virtue erratically, but nothing consistently without courage."

Lau-tzu uses four characters to write courage. Taken individually they mean; loving, causes, ability, and brave. He further explains, *"One of courage, with audacity, will die. One of courage, but gentle, spares death. From these two kinds of courage arise harm and benefit."* (Above sources on courage from Wikipedia)

Courage, therefore, needs to be seen in its "right" context. My prime concern is that those looking for this attribute in a leader not get confused or distracted by the notion popular in movies that courage is reckless.

Gordon Smith writes, "…true courage must be qualified by wisdom" (i.e. have wisdom as a partner). Smith also rationalizes that "true or genuine courage" is characterized by such virtues as gratitude, humility, patience, and moral integrity. In other words, "true courage" has "right partners."

On the contrary, if courage partners with "wrong partners" such as pride or audacity then trouble can be expected.

Obviously, Maya Angelou was referring to what we are calling "true courage" when she stated that courage is the virtue that enables other virtues.

So, when you are ***searching for courage*** in a prospective leader for your organization ***look specifically for the partners of courage*** that make it true and beneficial – wisdom, patience, humbleness, and honesty.

A comment on honesty and its relation to true courage…

I can recall, as perhaps you can, times when it seemed better to tell a lie, stretch the truth, and otherwise avoid being totally honest in order to seemingly avoid some fear in my heart. Finger pointing and avoidance of the truth (particularly as it pertains to me) is common in children. One of the important tasks of a parent is to train their children to be honest. As the years advance so too should courage mature and gain confidence to consistently be honest, tell the truth, and not be threatened by fear that inhibits courage.

Thus, besides looking for the partners of courage in a prospective leader, investigate as best you can how ***honest*** they are in various situations. This will help you access if courage has matured to the level of responsibility required.

Fear often causes us to do the wrong thing. Most often we fear for self. We lack the strength of character to do the right or courageous thing.

If you discern that a prospective candidate has a problem with honesty then it is highly likely they have a habit of allowing fear to override sound judgment. Such a person lacks the attribute of true courage.

The Apostle Paul gave his mentee Timothy great advice and en**courage**ment when he wrote, "For God did not give us a spirit of fear, but a spirit of power, of love, and of self-discipline." (2 Timothy 1:7)

We don't like to think of having a fearful spirit but, from my observations and experience, the threat of succumbing to fear is constant. I still find now at a mature age that I regularly need to recognize and confront that spirit of fear. I need to experience more and more of that spirit of power, love, and self-discipline that Paul refers to in order to counter fear and gain courage to be honest.

In summary, start the search for right or true courage in a person by:

1. Looking for the partners of courage and assessing how active they are in the life of your prospective leader (i.e. does the candidate consistently demonstrate such virtues as wisdom, patience, humbleness, and honesty). Remember, courage can arouse harm or benefit. It depends on the partners of courage;
2. Courage can and should develop and mature (honesty is a key measurement); and,
3. We can better understand true courage by comparing to its opposite – i.e. by comparing it to fear. (Example, fear can cause aggressive behaviour that may appear courageous but in fact could be self-centred in a response to fear.)

The reflective questions presented at the end of this epilogue should sharpen your perspective on courage and calling. I hope that you'll enjoy struggling with these and gaining clearer understandings of these important attributes of leaders.

But for now, I want to conclude this section on Courage and Calling, by sharing a memory of a gathering of some of folks who had lived through such a journey as told in the story Miracle …

It was after dinner and the business of the day's meetings. I was watching and listening. Perhaps I said something during the post dinner discourse but I can't recall. I do recall a time of jovial conversation with joking and playing with words. In the midst of this I, and other guests, were given a souvenir by the host. It was a necktie. The good mood continued and a couple of jokes ensued about the ties.

Then it happened – a surreal moment. Someone started to sing a line from an old hymn, "Blessed be the tie that binds." Spontaneously, and as if they had rehearsed for years, the entire group burst into song. The quality of the voices of the choir was pretty good but that is not what impressed on my memory. It was that picture of true fellowship; a group of friends who had all experienced horrific hardship now celebrating in song. One stanza of the hymn reads,

> "We share our mutual woes;
> Our mutual burdens bear;
> And often for each other flows
> The sympathizing tear."

They had indeed been subjected to hardship in great part due to their faith and their determination to be true to their calling. They chose to be examples of the spirit of power, love, and self-discipline – to be followers and disciples of Jesus without fear or apology. They had been tested by a time like few times before or after and they were the stronger for it. That night I witnessed a scene giving evidence to the fact that there is a wonderful "tie that binds."

Theirs was a song of victory and theirs was also a wonderful story of courage, conviction, and calling. One could almost see the partners of courage dancing and kicking fear out the door. The conviction to stay true to their calling was being celebrated and I, by the grace of God, was privileged to witness it.

Questions for Reflection and Further Study

1. Have you ever thoroughly considered the concept of "Calling," particularly as it applies to your life and vocation? Do you consider yourself a person pursuing a calling or callings? (I recommend to read the 2nd edition of Gordon T. Smith's book, "Courage and Calling – Embracing Your God Given Potential," as you consider your response)

2. Few people are fortunate to have a career that is also their vocational calling. Have you considered the difference? In your current situation do you have a career or job that is not a vocational calling? If so, can you identify your vocational calling? (Hint. It may well not be paid work.)

3. Was the information on courage helpful? Upon reflection could you now distinguish between reckless, aggressive actions that could be perceived as courageous and "true courage" that is triggered by "right reasons"?

4. What insights have you gained on courage? Write them down. Four references were given that you should refer to and reflect upon:

    a) The poem by George Farquhar;

    b) Gordon T. Smith's book;

    c) Quotes by renown persons; and,

    d) The Apostle Paul in his letter to Timothy (2 Timothy Ch 1 v 7)

    Have these contributed to your perspective?

5. Read the full story of David in the Bible (1 Samuel Ch 16 straight through to the end of 2 Samuel). How many years did David wait to be king from the time he was anointed by the Prophet Samuel until the people actually appointed him king? What "partners of courage" can you identify in David's ascent to the throne and his reign? Can you find any times where fear might have overcome his spirit of power, of love, and self-discipline and caused him to lie or make bad decisions?

6. Finally, apply insights from your reflection and learning from study to your life. Map out some resolutions for change that will help you improve the leadership attributes of Character, Courage, and Calling. I trust that your ongoing development in these areas will add to your contributions to family and society.

Prologue – A Mantra for Servant-Leaders

"Not To Be Served But To Serve"

———◆———

Jesus was walking throughout the countryside of Galilee with his disciples. Among the various topics of conversation of the disciples was one that centred on which one of them was the greatest.

When they had a chance to sit down, Jesus taught them saying, "If anyone wants to be first, he must be the very last, and the servant to all." (Mark 9: 35)

Sometime later, James and John asked Jesus whether they could sit at the right and left of him in glory. The other disciples heard of this request and became indignant with James and John (even though some had asked the question earlier about who would be the greatest).

Again, Jesus capitalized on a teachable moment by saying, "You know that those who are regarded as rulers of the Gentiles lord it over them, and their high officials exercise authority over them. Not so with you. Instead, whoever wants to be first must be slave of all. For even the Son of Man did not come to be served, but to serve, and to give his life as a ransom for many." (Mark 10: 42 to 45)

Story -
The Three Stewards Plan

———•✦•———

With the routine business on the board agenda complete, Chairman Andrew informed the directors that there was only one item of new business but it was critically important to the future of the organization. That statement aroused the curiosity of the twelve directors of Poverty Solutions International ("PSI"), a federation of local and national non-profit organizations ("NPO") that address issues relating to the expanding wealth gap and work toward alleviating poverty worldwide. The Chairman smiled and said, "Now that I've got your undivided attention, allow me to explain this rather unorthodox scheme that our CEO has proposed."

"But before I do that," continued Andrew, "I have an important announcement. "Julie, our CEO, has been our energetic, loyal, and capable leader for these past ten years. She has talked to me about resigning her post as CEO in order to take up a new venture that I will ask her to share with you later." Every eye was looking at Julie with head slightly bowed. The smile on her face reassured the directors that this was a planned and harmonious departure.

"With respect, Chairman," said Iris who was the director chairing the human resource committee and who was also familiar with the reason's for Julie's resignation notice, "Can we hear a little more from Julie? We'd love to hear what she has planned – and how we can help support."

"Of course," said Chairman Andrew quickly as he looked at CEO Julie and gestured for her to speak.

Julie started by stating how grateful she was to have been given the opportunity to serve PSI as its CEO and how gratifying the past ten years had been to her professionally and how much she had enjoyed working with the members of the board and colleagues to address the many and various issues of poverty in the world today. "I'll elaborate on details another time," she said, "But for now it is suffice to say that I'll be pursuing a doctorate in economics at the London School of Economics starting fifteen months from now. I will focus my research and present a thesis on the importance of the G20 implementing policies that attack poverty and foster sustainable development of the 3rd world."

She was bursting with excitement and starting to elaborate as the Chairman gently interrupted, "I had reserved dinner for chatting about Julie's future." He looked at Julie apologetically and added in a lighthearted tone, "And I understand that you can all join us because I'm privy to your flight schedules." He concluded, "We all look forward to that time of fellowship. For now I would like to discuss an idea with you on how we might fill the very capable shoes of Julie by the time she departs to London in a year or so."

Andrew now took on a businesslike demeanor as he started to speak, "As I prefaced, the scheme we are about to present now in an effort to identify a successor for Julie is a bit unorthodox. I haven't heard of such a process before but as Julie and I talked it through I became convinced and now confident that it could work."

"You have our attention again," said the Treasurer. "I hope it doesn't cost too much."

Chairman Andrew chuckled, as did the other directors as

they often joked with their prudent treasurer. The Chairman then settled everyone down. "Ok, we've had a long afternoon so without further ado, and foolishness, I will ask Julie to explain the idea for your consideration."

Julie followed the cue and began, "As you all know, we have three executives working with us who are all very likely to apply for CEO of PSI once it is made public that I am leaving and once a search committee and process is set up to select my replacement. I believe that some or all of you prefer that this vacancy be filled internally."

Julie was interrupted by one of the board members at this point as she asked the Chairman, "Can we discuss first whether we search internally or externally before we predetermine that we are limiting our selection to an internal candidate?"

Chairman Andrew responded that he intended to address that issue after Julie had a chance to present the plan. "But," he said, "As the matter has been brought up, can I have a show of hands of who prefer an internal candidate? Provided of course they are able to prove themselves capable to be CEO of this organization," he added.

The hands of most of the directors raised giving Andrew confidence to proceed. "Ok then. Let's have Julie explain further. I'll wrap up and entertain questions at the end of her presentation." Chairman Andrew then invited Julie to continue.

"Well, to be clear, this proposal does not rule out considering an external candidate but does provide for a testing of the leadership capabilities of our current executives. Even if the Board is not satisfied and decide that none of the three internal candidates should be appointed, we will know a lot more about them and their ability to lead," opened Julie as she glanced at the faces around the board room table.

"You have our attention again," said the Treasurer to

which Julie quipped back, "And, the plan has a great payback for PSI." Julie continued through the chuckling, "I propose that we restructure PSI operations for the duration of this appraisal exercise at least, whereby we put each of our executives in charge of one of the three geographical areas where we presently engage in development work. I propose Joseph oversee Africa, Juan Diego oversee Asia, and Michael oversee Latin America." Seeing the questioning expressions around the room she quickly addressed them by saying, "Yes, I wanted to neutralize the ethnic background and language advantages and thus have the three men rely more on other capabilities. The restructure will be on an eight-month trial period during which time I will be making comprehensive assessments of their progress. Each will have a baseline set and then I'll measure how they perform in various areas to advance sustainable economic and community development in the areas where we work." Julie then went through details of the plan on the PowerPoint.

The Chairman thanked Julie and entertained questions. There were a few questions on the assessment criteria that were addressed by Julie and Iris. Besides being chair of the HR committee, Iris was also an accomplished HR professional. Her support added to the credibility of the proposal.

There was one question as to whether the executive for finance and administration would be disadvantaged by the criteria for performance that was biased on operations. Julie addressed this question by explaining in more detail the expectations for a CEO of an organization such as PSI, which included both administrative and operational capabilities. "He would have to prove himself in operations and in general leadership if he were to handle the responsibilities of CEO for PSI," she said, then added, "And, don't forget, there are two other executives under review, one of which also has little or no operational experience."

Finally, some board members questioned again the ethnic and language mix. Surely PSI would benefit by having a person of Chinese background looking after Asia area, a Hispanic overseeing Latin American operations, and an African American in charge of Africa. "Don't forget that we are looking for an internal candidate who can serve as the next CEO," said Chairman Andrew in defense of Julie's argument, "As CEO, the person will have to lead an organization that works in many countries of the world." Approving nods were apparent around the table prodding the Chairman to ask if there were any more questions. There being no further questions or comments, he then suggested that there was consensus to proceed with the "Three Stewards Plan." Hands raised in affirmation of his assumption of consensus. The Chair then declared it a resolution and authorized Julie to proceed with the plan's implementation.

Chairman Andrew instructed the board members that they were to leave the execution of the plan in Julie's hands. He also emphasized the need for confidentiality. He then adjourned the meeting and reminded directors of the dinner, a couple of hours hence, where they would hear more of Julie's future plans.

Julie did share her future plans at the dinner that turned out to be a wonderful time of fellowship. The directors fully enjoyed the food, conversation, and company. Julie did however take the opportunity to converse separately with two directors who did not appear to be sold on her scheme. She was successful in getting confirmation from them that they would not interfere with the execution of the plan.

Most of the directors resided out of town. Julie had an early and leisurely breakfast at the hotel with them and saw each one onto the shuttle to the airport at various times according to their flight departures. By noon she had completed her farewells and headed home to relax and also to take stock and pray about how to approach the three executives and set the stewards plan in motion.

On Monday Julie followed her normal routine at the office that included a session with her leadership team for operational briefings and inspiration time. She briefed the team on the outcomes of the recent board meeting, including the decision to restructure. She did not elaborate on the details that affected the three executives but gave enough information to make the entire team feel comfortable with the upcoming change. She set separate appointment times with her "three stewards" where she intended to explain the restructure plan in detail.

Julie met separately with each of the three executives. She gave each a folder with details that explained the restructure, how it affected them specifically, and even a stock take of the region for which they would be responsible. The latter information provided a starting point on which they were expected to build. She explained that the rest was up to them. She stated that she would be available to answer questions and support but Julie made sure to emphasize that she would not do the work for them. "This is your baby and we want to see how you nurture it," said Julie metaphorically to each executive. She wasn't surprised that each one had different reactions and responses to the change.

Joseph, who was in charge of finance and administration, appeared keen and spoke confidently of his abilities and the chance to show Julie and the Board what he could achieve in this new role. He asked a lot of questions. Some questions were for clarification, which Julie answered. When questions entered the "Not doing it for you" zone, Julie would turn it back to Joseph and remind him to take initiative and even risk if that is what he purposed to do. Julie concluded the meeting with a statement, "Joseph, you should now go and prepare your business plan. As explained, I will need a copy of it when ready for the record. I will not comment on it unless it is putting PSI at undue risk in which case I'll exert my authority and change it. Otherwise, you have a budget and can work out your plan within those boundaries." She then shook hands with Joseph, wished him good luck, and opened the door for him to leave.

Juan Diego was responsible for development, which for PSI primarily meant raising funds from donations. He also was in charge of some related activities such as public relations, branding, social media, and research. He was a good fit for his portfolio of responsibility and a fine example of a modern sales and marketing executive. While he was comfortable working with people and even energized by social interaction, he knew the value of information based decision- making and set his strategies and action plans accordingly. Like Joseph, Juan Diego did not have operational experience with PSI but he was anxious to learn and take on the challenge of being responsible for formulating and executing a plan to facilitate community development in the Asian region. Julie gave the same closing instructions to Juan Diego as she had with Joseph when time came for the meeting to end. She saw him do a fist pump as he quickly walked back to his office.

Michael was full of confidence as he entered Julie's office. He was currently in charge of operations at PSI and felt this experience could be put to good use if given the chance to take on more responsibility. His confidence was shaken a little when Julie informed him that he would be responsible to develop the Latin American region. His shortcomings in Spanish language and Hispanic culture caused him to suddenly be uncomfortable and he questioned the wisdom of the restructure plan. However, once Julie elaborated on the restructure strategy and encouraged him, Michael recovered from his insecurity and expressed that he was keen to take on the challenge. He had a good track record of fieldwork and had a lot of strengths for undertaking a task such as the one before him. He and Julie had an invigorating talk as Michael shared his hopes and aspirations to further the prospects for sustainability of the development projects that PSI had undertaken in the Latin American area. Julie looked at her watch. "I didn't realize that we talked so long," she said, "I have another meeting that I can't reschedule so let's conclude for today. I look forward to reviewing your business plan when it is ready."

"When is the deadline for that again," asked Michael.

"Deadlines are up to you Michael. This is your project. I know that you'll do a good job." Michael was keen to start. He smiled and thanked Julie then moved quickly to call a meeting with his team.

Julie hadn't envisioned the emotions that the plan would evoke from her. In all her years at PSI she had been fully engaged in all the affairs of the organization. That is certainly not to imply that she micro managed her executives or used a domineering leadership style. In fact she had a collaborative leadership approach and devoted much time and effort to developing effective teams. This style caused her to be engaged in conversation with members of her leadership teams on a daily basis. Giving her three executives full autonomy for the projects they had been assigned caused her to be outside of the day-to-day discussions and decision-making processes. However, as part of the process, Julie had implemented a good mechanism whereby she received reports and feedback on the activities and use of PSI's resources, thus she was well informed. But the fact that she was more of an observer than an important member of the team made her uncomfortable. Noting the adverse impact the change was having on her, Julie countered by using the extra time to focus on the evaluation and reports that she would need to give the Board by the end of the eight-month project period.

As the plan moved into the second half of the trial period Julie already had a mountain of documentation with details of progress submitted by the three executives and from her own observations and data. She realized that she needed to find an effective way to communicate the findings and outcomes to the directors on the board. Too much information and paper would run the risk that the directors would not read the report or be able to absorb all the information in it if they did. Too little and surely board members would have a list of questions for her. Julie spent a good deal of time conducting research on the art and science of preparing succinct and effective personnel talent reports and, when she had finally drafted a template, she asked a couple of experts to vet her work. After a couple of months she was satisfied that she had a framework that would allow her to present a 4 to 5 page report on each of the three "stewards."

While being careful not to interfere, Julie did need to converse with each of the three executives on a regular basis. This was fully acceptable to the three executives as they realized that Julie was still responsible to the Board and PSI stakeholders for the well being of the organization. On one such occasion, she noticed that Michael and Juan Diego were spending quite a bit of time meeting in each other's office. She had also noticed them meeting over lunch periodically. She took the chance to bring the matter up at one of their progress meetings. Both men were very open and consistent in their response. They had decided to collaborate and share ideas and resources to develop their respective areas. Moreover, Michael had been taking Spanish lessons and would spend a few minutes most days practicing on Juan Diego. Julie thought this was a good thing and within the rules of the plan but did ask whether they ever met with Joseph. "Oh yes, we all lunch together once a week when we are all in town," they would both similarly reply, "Conversation is all very cordial but Joseph doesn't talk about any happenings in the African area." Julie thought that feedback a bit strange as she received progress reports from Joseph regularly. The information did cause her to be suspicious however and she determined to seek out corroboration of the information in Joseph's reports. In fact, she decided, it would be prudent to ensure reports of all three of the executives were verifiable by third parties.

As the Three Stewards Plan moved into the seventh month Julie began applying information to her report templates. She had also arranged for on-site visits to PSI's community development partners in Asia, Africa, and Latin America. This was quite a logistical venture that would understandably involve a good deal of travel, time, and energy. However, Julie was not one to present such important reports to the Board without meeting with the partners face-to-face. Of course, she had conversed with a number of the overseas leaders and staff by phone, email, and skype but, to be complete, she needed to make the visits. This road trip would take a full month of Julie's time.

The site visits were very enlightening indeed, not to mention emotionally demanding. As a caring professional, Julie experienced the satisfaction of witnessing the good progress of many of the partner communities in sustainable development, the joy of seeing life improvement in the lives of people, and sharing happy, playful times with children. There was a real sense that PSI was making a significant difference in these communities. There were also emotionally draining times when Julie shared in the pain and grief of some community members. Most disturbing, however, was the discovery that some of the positive outputs reported in the African area were at best public relation exaggerations and worse, a couple were pure fabrications.

The Board had scheduled their quarterly meeting a few

days before the end of the predetermined eight-month trial period of the restructure. The process of the Three Stewards Plan called for each of the executives to present their own report. Julie would not present her report until all three of the executives made their presentations to the Board. Chairman Andrew knew that receiving six hours of reports would be exhausting but he also realized that directors would not want to bear the suspense of waiting until the next day for Julie's report. He was also concerned that some directors might form unbalanced opinions based on the reports received by the three executives. Moreover, while the final process for selection of Julie's successor had not been determined, it would be natural for directors to discuss this matter at social time and even inadvertently lobby for one or another of the candidates. The chairman therefore decided to have an early light dinner scheduled late afternoon and thereafter afford Julie time to present her report on the same day as the three executives.

Leaders of non-profit organizations tend to be very enthusiastic about their work. Chairman Andrew was well aware of this and the likelihood for time overruns thus instructed each candidate in advance that they would be given a time warning 30 minutes prior to the conclusion of their 2-hour session. To their credit, all three executives had put a good deal of thought and effort into their presentations to get their message across within the time parameters. Following the question and answer portion of each presentation Chairman Andrew would declare a twenty-minute break.

Michael was the first to present. He introduced his report in Spanish to preface how much he appreciated the opportunity to head up the leadership of the challenging Latin American region. Board members were impressed that he had tackled all the sustainable development targets previously established in PSI's strategic plan even though they all realized that the long-term investment nature of this approach made his growth statistics less impressive. Michael had conducted a tremendous amount of research, consulted all the leaders and a number of other stakeholders at partner communities, and surveyed donors and sustainable development experts before constructing his action plan. He engaged leaders and community members in executing the plan and it was obvious from the testimonials that a movement was underway to solve the poverty issues that were present there. He was also successful in engaging leaders of community development sectors in talks and processes. This included leaders in government, education, industry, religion, and non-profit associations. There was growth in some important areas too, including the number of donors and dollars raised. Michael had also mobilized "expertise twinning" whereby accomplished professionals in engineering, medicine, water management, and dentistry were encouraged to forge long-term relationships for mutual support in development.

Juan Diego was next. His experience in public speaking and presentation was obvious and he had leveraged on his strengths in fund-raising to generate impressive growth in financial support of the partner projects. What really impressed the Board in this regard however was the number of donors from Asia that he had been able to enlist. Moreover, the activity plan to recruit more support there looked very credible, particularly in light of the success that he had had in a mere eight months. Added to these impressive numbers were his efforts at addressing the longer-term development issues. This part of the plan looked surprisingly similar to Michael's and when asked about this by one of the directors, Juan was very open with the fact that he had discussed those matters with Michael and other experts prior to formulating his operational plan. Juan Diego concluded his presentation with testimonials from those on the ground in partner communities that were sincere and touching. The professional attention to detail in the production of the presentation and testimonials was obvious and impressive even though most directors expected this from Juan Diego.

Joseph entered the room dressed in tradition African garb given to him by one of the partners. He knew that the directors had just finished two long presentations and he tried to lighten the mood with a couple of jokes and even had them stand and try a Zulu dance step. This was successful in getting the blood flowing and engaging the directors in lighthearted verbal interchange. Joseph kept the lighthearted approach throughout the presentation except for a couple of times where he injected some heart tugging emotion. The testimonials were all very supportive of Joseph's efforts and the growth charts that he presented were most impressive. The presentation was briefer than the other two affording the board members more time for questions. During question time it became apparent to most directors that while Joseph tried to project an aura of competence his business plan and it's execution lacked the integrity and thoroughness of Michael and Juan Diego's. When all the questions where exhausted, Chairman Andrew thanked Joseph and dismissed him.

Andrew looked at the clock and noted that they had made up thirty minutes on Joseph's presentation. He informed the directors that as the schedule for their early dinner had been fixed he would declared the meeting adjourned a little earlier than expected and to be reconvened at 6:00 pm sharp. The directors welcomed this recess, many of them already checking email and other messages.

Julie was given the floor once the meeting was reconvened. She thanked the chairman for arranging a light dinner so that directors would not have cause to slumber. It was obvious amidst the smiles and chuckles however that the directors were most attentive and anxious to see and hear what Julie had prepared.

"What you saw from the presentations of Michael and Juan Diego is more or less what you get in terms of their personalities and capabilities," Julie opened as she presented her findings on Michael and then Juan Diego. "The primary object of this eight-month exercise was to challenge all three gentlemen to perform and also for me to measure that performance," she continued, "Both of these men approached the challenge professionally and executed their business plan with integrity and humility. The latter attribute allowed them to collaborate with ease and form highly effective plans. The site visits that I conducted last month allowed me to affirm with confidence that what was presented to you was accurate and true. I am indeed proud to say that after eight short months our partners in Asia and Latin America are optimistic that there are getting the support they need to find solutions to take them out of poverty. Our organization is about mobilizing and matching resourceful people to fight and defeat poverty. These two men understand this and have done a commendable job." Julie then shared the summary of detailed information that she had gathered, correlated, and plotted in the different categories on a pro forma that she referred to as the "Capabilities Grid."

There were a few mini-meetings emerging around the table. Directors were obviously pleased with the performance of Michael and Juan Diego. Chairman Andrew spoke up to restore order and reminded directors that Julie had yet to report on the "third steward."

Quiet was restored and Julie projected her Capabilities Grid onto the screen for Joseph. "I was a bit surprised with Joseph's performance too," she opened, "But in a different way than our other two stewards." She referred to her written notes and continued, "While Joseph did not have any direct operational experience at the beginning of the pilot project, he, as a member of the leadership team, was able to receive indirect experience of operations. Moreover, prior to the plan being formulated, Joseph had intimated to me on a number of occasions that he would do well at operations. Furthermore, during the initial interview when I explained the restructure, Joseph spoke confidently that he would be more than capable to do a good job."

Julie paused for a moment as she shuffled her notes. The room was quiet and all eyes were on her as she continued to speak. "However, that confidence did not materialize into performance. You saw from Joseph's presentation that he lacks knowledge on matters of poverty and solutions to alleviate it. He relied on building relationship with key leaders in the African area by channeling more donated dollars and goods through them personally. By doing so he had put temptation in their way and corrupted PSI's service delivery system. We need to ensure as much integrity in our operations as possible and we need to nurture right character in leaders throughout the organization. I was also able to determine beyond doubt that our partners in Africa have become more dependent over these eight months and less able to be self-sufficient in finding their way out of poverty." Julie lifted her eyes and glanced around the room to witness uncomfortable body language. PSI had long since abandoned activities that created dependency in favour of those that fostered mutual support for self-sustainable development. Julie took a breath and concluded, " Thus, for whatever reason, be it naivety, lack of knowledge, or shallowness of character, Joseph could not perform at the standard expected of a senior leader in PSI."

Julie's report together with Joseph's lackluster presentation had certainly eliminated him as a CEO candidate in the minds of most directors. There were a few directors though, with whom Joseph had forged trusting relationship that were rather shaken by the revelation of Joseph's lack of stewardship and leadership qualities. The Treasurer, who had probably spent the most time with Joseph when he was in charge of finance, was trying to manage his emotion as he harshly asked of Julie, "How could you have worked with this man for over a year and not noticed his failings?"

Chairman Andrew was concerned with the tone of the question and started to comment but Julie interrupted and accepted the question by saying, "That is a good and also a fair question. This is obviously a case where academic and professional qualification in accountancy does not give assurances of good leadership or stewardship. This restructure challenge revealed this. When in a subordinate role reporting to me and as a member of our leadership team, the accountability structure and integrity of others kept Joseph performing within acceptable standards. However, when given more autonomy and authority to lead an entire area, the weaknesses in character and capability were exposed. The good news for PSI is that the Three Stewards Plan has given the Board a tremendous amount of information about the three men under review."

Chairman Andrew interjected by saying, "Thank you Julie. Indeed, we have a good amount of reliable and accurate information on which to guide our discussions as we go forward as a Board. It is a good time to show our appreciation to Julie for proposing this experiment and for her long, dedicated, and distinguished service to PSI." His comments evoked applause and spontaneous comments of acclamation and affirmation.

When the demonstration of appreciation subsided Chairman Andrew spoke up and said, "It has been a very long day. I thank you all for you perseverance. Again, thank you Julie for your terrific leadership to PSI." Applause interrupted his concluding remarks.

When quiet was restored, a smiling chairman finished his comments, "Before we adjourn, I propose that we shortlist both Michael and Juan Diego for consideration as our next chief executive and authorize the search committee headed by Iris to prepare a selection process for the Board's consideration. I further propose that the Board authorize me to work with Julie to deal with Joseph."

The vote was unanimous.

Epilogue – Capability – The Essential Attribute for Accepted Leadership

The final story in the trilogy focuses on ***Capability or Competency*** for any task demanding leadership. I will use these words interchangeable as we examine the fourth essential attribute of leadership.

I am confident to state that there will not be a day of the year pass without some person or committee in a NPO or other social sector institution looking to recruit leadership in support of their cause. The scene in the boardroom in this story is not unusual. The scheme devised by CEO Julie is somewhat unusual in my experience but not because boards do not look internally for a replacement of an exiting CEO but because the examination of the three internal prospects was so systematic and thorough.

Let's have a closer look at this approach for executive search.

It was obvious that CEO Julie was a very capable and respected leader. If she did not command respect from her Board and if she did not have a supportive chairman this plan would never have gotten off the ground. It is not clear whether the questioning of the proposed Three Stewards

Plan from certain members of the board was simply due diligence or whether there were doubting members trying to exert influence and squash the plan. Given the complex dynamics of voluntary boards, it would not be unusual for either of those reasons and more to account for the questioning. Respected as she was, Julie needed the support of the chairman of the board and a few other influential directors if the Three Stewards Plan was to get approval to proceed.

I trust that you got the message that the search for Julie's replacement was going to be thorough, systematic, and professional. The chairman cautioned members of the board rather firmly that they were duty bound to ensure confidentiality and to avoid any kind of interference or impropriety. If the plan was to have any chance at success it required members of the board to be professional and do their duty, regardless of how friendly they might be with any of the three internal candidates.

The professional effort that Julie put into the systems for analysis and data collection was substantial. The systems were designed to be unbiased, relevant, and clear to communicate. Like a top international athlete, Julie made a complex and painstaking effort look effortless when the time came for the presentation at the end of the trial period.

And, what was Julie (and Chairman Andrew and Iris, Chair of HR Committee) looking for in a prospective CEO?

This brings us to the matter of identifying important capabilities of successful chief executives of social sector institutions. They need to possess a combination of skills and qualities that allow them to build effective and sustainable learning organizations. These essential skills and qualities express themselves in two broad ways; one, a style of leadership and, two, a strong belief in team play or teamwork and its contribution to building a learning organization.

First, some comments on leadership style…

Renowned management consultant, author, and researcher Jim Collins has championed the idea of what he calls "Level 5 Leadership" in CEOs of organizations, particularly social sector institutions such as NPOs, hospitals, and colleges. He has compiled ample and compelling data to justify statements such as the one he wrote in the Harvard Business Review, *"Good-to-Great Transformations Don't Happen Without Level 5 Leaders at the Helm. They just don't."*

So what is Level 5 Leadership?

The title of Collin's article in the HBR gives us a clue, "Level 5 Leadership: The Triumph of Humility and Fierce Resolve." He sums up his observations as follows, "A level 5 executive builds enduring greatness (for the organization) through a paradoxical combination of personal humility plus professional will." He notes as well that while level 5 leaders possess these characteristics they have also developed other competencies such as knowledge, skills, good work habits, and the ability to work effectively with other people.

There is much more for talent recruiters to learn from Collins and the profile of level 5 leaders but it is suffice to note in our Three Stewards Plan story that retiring CEO Julie, Chairman Andrew, and Search Executive Iris were hopeful to see these level-5 leadership qualities revealed in all three internal candidates or, failing that, at least in one of them.

And they did. But before I comment on that, let's better understand the second broad capability that they were looking for and that was the prospective candidate's commitment to teamwork and other disciplines that cultivate learning organizations.

Understanding how to create and maintain a learning organization…

Recall how easily Juan Diego and Michael were able to

collaborate and cooperate in the best interest of PSI and its client communities. They were less concerned about themselves and more focused on how to achieve sustainable targets and contribute to the success of PSI and its work. The story also revealed some of their talents, knowledge, and good work habits. Moreover, both were humble enough to readily acknowledge that they needed to acquire new skills in order to achieve their goals. They chose to learn from each other plus glean information from experts who could help them formulate a professional plan.

In his book "The Fifth Discipline – The Art & Practice of The Learning Organization," Peter Senge points to five contributors for development of learning organizations; Shared Vision, Mental Models, Personal Mastery, Teamwork, and Systems Thinking. The CEO is in the best position to stimulate and encourage these contributors. The effort needed to sustain ongoing learning in any organization and effectively advance its mission is significant. These efforts also must be directed and consistent. It is essential that a leader genuinely believe that investing in people today will reap long-tem benefits. Learning organizations are not built overnight. It takes vision, energy, talent, and commitment to cultivate such organizations.

Michael and Juan Diego intuitively understood the qualities and skills that are needed to effectively lead a social institution and build learning communities. The story paints a picture of them engaging people in both the North and the South to construct a foundation that future generations could build on. This is visionary leadership that is humble enough to sacrifice short-term results in order to gain long-term benefits for our children and grandchildren.

Michael and Juan Diego would need to have these qualities and skills nurtured and developed of course but they

Epilogue – Capability

were showing obvious leadership potential for their organization, Poverty Solutions International.

Joseph, on the other hand, lacked many of these qualities. While he was good at hobnobbing and projecting an aura of competency, he actually was ineffective at working with people. It was all about him, not others, or the organization. He desperately wanted to be recognized by others as a capable leader but in fact his character was too shallow to handle that level of responsibility. While appearing to be humble he in fact had a superiority belief that appeared periodically when he took opportunity to criticize others. Joseph was always looking for the sand in the eye of others while ignoring the log in his own eye. Such a person is incapable of generating the team effort needed to build successful organizations. Moreover, he lacked vision for the work of PSI and his understanding for how to further its poverty alleviation aspirations was shallow. Thus it would be impossible for him to cultivate the kind of organization that PSI felt called to be.

Hard work but a good result for The Three Stewards Plan…

The plan was not only successful at identifying two candidates for the soon to be vacant CEO post but it also identified the lack of leadership and deficiency for teamwork in one person. Julie's plan had given the Board the information that they required to go forward. While some were feeling sorry for Joseph, everyone was happy with the results of the Three Stewards Plan.

Well, perhaps not everyone was happy.

Recall the reaction of the Treasurer. He was obviously taken in by Joseph's charm and feeling quite embarrassed when his horse finished last. He directed this embarrassment and resentment at CEO Julie. Chairman Andrew accurately judged the comments as out of line and quickly moved to diffuse a prospective bomb. But, demonstrating her level 5 leader qualities, Julie humbly but firmly responded and competently put the matter to rest.

Perhaps you can read the story again and see if you can identify more capabilities and qualities in Juan Diego and Michael that position them to develop toward level 5 leaders; those seemingly paradoxical qualities of humility combined with professional will. Perhaps too you'll identify the capabilities that enable Michael and Juan Diego to be cultivators of learning organizations.

While qualities that contribute toward level 5 leadership will certainly position the leader to navigate the complexities of a social sector institution and cultivate corporate cultures able to sustain learning organizations, she or he must demonstrate their competence if their leadership is going to be genuinely accepted by peers and subordinates.

Pat MacMillan, founder of Team Resources and author of "The Performance Factor – Unlocking the Secrets of Teamwork," writes, "High performance teams need clear, competent leadership. When such leadership is lacking, groups loose their way."

Anyone who had been a member of a team in any arena, be it sports, commerce, or community project, understands this concept immediately. If members of a team are truly going to accept the leadership of an appointed team leader, that leader must be able to show that they are competent.

I am confident that you not only appreciated Juan Diego and Michael's style of leadership and abilities to work well with people but also noted their competency to advance the vision and mission of PSI. The scheme that Julie planned gave them a working theatre to demonstrate their competency. The majority of the board members recognized that both Michael and Juan Diego were competent in the work of PSI and this conclusion was based on real and reliable facts. The latter is critically important to making right decisions.

I highly recommend reading Jim Collins, Peter Senge, and Pat MacMillan. Their articles and books provide clear and compelling arguments on the type of leaders who are successful at building viable, effective, teams and sustainable learning organizations.

Don't miss the point…it will cost your organization.

I feel convicted to add this serious note. If search committees or professional recruiters make a wrong selection at the CEO level in a social sector institution, it will be very costly to the organization in many ways. Frankly, getting it wrong is likely to launch the demolition of the organization. Rather than spending your time, energy, and resources on constructive effort that builds your organization from "Good to Great," you will find yourself constantly mending crumbling foundations that took painstaking efforts and years to construct. It is truly heartbreaking to witness the erosion of an organization's work and reputation because of a wrong hire at the CEO level.

Yet, despite a search committee and board's best efforts, wrong hires at the CEO level will occur. If policy or governance leaders find themselves in this situation the best advice is to right the wrong immediately.

Questions for Reflection and Further Study

1. Have you ever worked with or reported to a colleague who is not competent at their job or who otherwise lacks leadership for their role? Or, to the contrary, worked with a very capable leader? How would you compare your experiences with both those scenarios?
2. Would you agree with Pat MacMillan's statement, "High performance teams need clear, competent leadership. When such leadership is lacking, groups loose their way"? If so, to what degree? Can you think of any situation where unclear, incompetent leadership led a team to victory? (Or, an organization, country, etc to success)
3. What virtues or character traits would you say a leader must possess to be slotted into what Jim Collins calls level-5 leadership? Do you feel that someone can work to develop these if they are lacking?
4. Much has been written about "Servant Leadership," although I did not make reference to any in this book. However, do you see a link with the mantra in the prologue and your understanding of a) servant leadership; and, b) level-5 leadership?
5. Would you consider the organization that you work for now to be classified as a "Learning Organization" in the way Peter Senge describes? What advantages do you see of such an organization culture over one that does not practice all 5 disciplines that Senge identifies?

6. Of the three stewards, and what you know of them from the story, which one would you prefer to work with and why?

7. Each of the three stories referred to "testing" in some form. How do you feel about purposefully testing people in both life and work situations?

8. When reading the three stories, did you notice the linkage of the four essential attributes of leaders? If you were asked to place these four attributes in a "recommended order of attainment" for leadership development, how would you order and why? (E.g. Capability then courage, calling, and character.) Or, would you say that there is no such thing as a "recommended order of attainment"?

Summary, Practices & Tools, and References

Summing up the Stories and the Search for the Four Essential Attributes of Successful Social Sector Leaders

———•———

While the three stories each intended to highlight one or two of the four essential attributes for the purpose of instruction, all four are, in fact, intimately linked. John, for example, could not move forward in character development until he stopped wandering and start the search for his callings. His journey would require true courage (and development of its partners) to help him pursue calling and develop character and capabilities. Thus, while for analytic and evaluation purposes the four attributes will involve separation, in practice, the four attributes reside together in leadership growth.

Those tasked with enlisting talent into an organization must look for the right depth and combination of Character, Courage, Calling, and Capability in a person assigned for leadership, regardless of the responsibility level of the post. Candidates deficient in one attribute may well be lacking in others. Take care to know as much as you can about leadership candidates, even to the extent of "getting into their feet."

Everyone in the organization should be encouraged to develop his or her leadership potential. Leadership development programs must include character development.

Calling, in my view, is the least understood, and certainly the least sought after attribute of leaders – by both recruiters and the individual leader candidates themselves. More attention needs to be given to this attribute for, if better understood, it offers the promise of real satisfaction in life and vocation, and also consistent integrity in leadership.

Capability should be viewed in a broad sense with the prime objective being to have one's leadership genuinely accepted by peers and subordinates. Thus, recruiters should not overvalue any single contributor to one's capability (e.g. academic qualifications) but rather should consider a mix of competencies that collectively contribute to accepted leadership.

An organization is composed of individuals from a wide spectrum of backgrounds. They will bring their whole past into your organization. Can this past and their individualism be transformed into effective teams? This is an important question for recruiters. Due attention and resources must be given to talent search and selection processes, and development programs to ensure that the four essential attributes of leaders can be nurtured and enabled to contribute toward teamwork in the best interest of the organization.

Certainly a CEO is in a position that can do the most good for the organization, or, to the contrary, can inflict the most harm. For this reason extra care and diligence needs to be taken when searching for and selecting a CEO. Search committees should give due attention to personality traits and competencies that contribute to what Jim Collins terms Level 5 Leadership. These traits and competencies, I believe, also position the CEO to cultivate a Learning Organization. Certainly, to the competencies of successful leaders of social institutions that have been identified by such experts as Collins, MacMillan and Senge, the search committee needs to ensure that the candidate:

- Have sufficient depth and strength of "right character";
- Possess "true courage";
- Be "called" as a leader for the job and work; and,
- Demonstrate "professional competency" at least at a level sufficient to gain genuine support for their leadership.

Bear in mind however that, while the CEO sets the tone, it needs to be recognized and appreciated that other staff and volunteers contribute to the mission and vision of the organization. They deliver the programs and services, and forge the personal relationships that express your mission to clients. Staff and volunteers also administer the affairs of your organization and otherwise support your cause. Collectively the contribution of each and every stakeholder is significant and meaningful.

Those tasked with recruiting talent into an organization and those responsible for nurturing and managing that talent should themselves receive ongoing training in the art and science of character and leadership development.

A factor that distinguishes great organizations from mediocre or even good ones is their consistent and professional attention to developing the human potential of staff and volunteers. They spend time and invest resources to train and develop their people and then expect that the collective contributions of those people will impact on the organization's mission and vision. A critically important ingredient in the recipe for cultivating reputable organizations is a consistent and comprehensive plan for character development

I don't add the importance of developing the character

and leadership abilities of line service staff and support workers frivolously. Ongoing attention to the professional development of every person engaged in an organization's mission and genuine efforts to direct that collective talent and energy toward that end is, in my experience, critically important for those intent on building highly effective and reputable organizations.

Leaders should also realize that a wrong hire, or volunteer enlistment, will cause pain and be a drag on your organization's resources. We found in the story of the three stewards that wrong, or at least ineffective hires, can and do occur at senior levels as well as more junior levels. Leaders should not ignore this reality and be trained to deal effectively with such situations.

Finally, a recap statement, perhaps to post near your work area as a guiding principle:

Leaders of social sector institutions who aspire to develop "great" organizations must give considerable attention to find ways and means of enlisting in their fold people of integrity and upright character who are truly courageous and able to discern and accept their calling in life and vocation, and who are committed to continually develop capability or competence for their calling.

Practices and Tools to Help Leaders Identify and Develop Character, Courage, Calling, and Competency and Cultivate Learning Organizations

---

Two Basics...

1. Activate "Human Resource Guidance Control Systems"

Searching for and enlisting talent into an organization is not just the job of a HR department. Indeed, as we have seen in the story of the Three Stewards Plan, a search committee commissioned by the Board is appropriate and common when recruiting a CEO. Moreover, a scan of your organization will more than likely reveal that quite a few other people are involved in recruitment activity, either formally or informally.

For example, a board member may ask a friend to join a committee, line staff may be responsible to recruit volunteers or part-time staff, and campaigns will be conducted to recruit sponsors, members, or support partners. In the absence of considered parameters to guide recruitment one is purely dependant on luck to make a good hire or enlistment.

It is therefore essential that Board and Management ensure that there are mechanisms in place that "guide recruitment" and "control risks." Mechanisms at the disposal of governors and managers include policies, systems, procedures, and practices. Leaders need to ensure that such mechanisms are sufficient to guide and control everyone involved in recruitment and subsequent professional development efforts.

Collectively I term these mechanisms as "HR Guidance Control Systems." If designed and utilized effectively they will both guide the human development efforts in your organization and also reduce the risk of misadventure. A detailed discussion on the ways and means of providing such "guidance control systems" is beyond the scope of this book but leaders are well advised to insist that systems are not only in place but that they are subject to regular review and continual improvement.

2. Design and Implement a Plan to Cultivate Learning Communities

In my view, human resource development ("HRD") is the most important activity for any organization; and, it is the key target for leaders if they aspire to nurture a learning organization. Take care not to overlook that HRD begins even before a person joins your organization. Good staff hires and recruitment of volunteers makes a huge difference to the effectiveness of an organization in pursuing mission. If you recruit the "wrong" person, you will expend a disproportionate amount of time, energy, and resources on that person; and, this errant expenditure of energy will undoubtedly rob "right" enlistments from the attention they deserve.

This principle applies to paid staff of any classification (FT, PT, Casual) and also to volunteers. You want to recruit the right people for the right roles.

Practices and Tools

I recall my Warrant Officer drilling into his recruits the premise that time spent on reconnaissance is never wasted when it comes to formulating and executing a plan. I believe the same principle holds for executing HRD plans. Take the time and make the effort to get reliable, accurate information when formulating your plan. Then, the ultimate execution of your plan will have a much better chance for success.

While I have given a summary of summaries for these two foundational efforts to build great organizations, the actual forming and executing of detailed plans to activate HR guidance control systems and cultivate a learning organization culture will take significant time, attention, and energy of a CEO and his or her leadership team. Leaders should not underestimate the importance that clear, consistent, and reasoned policies, procedures, practices, systems, and positive working cultures are to the workforce in social sector institutions.

Some Tools for Recruiting and Cultivating Talent

Guidance control systems and HRD plans require kits with appropriate "tools" for maintenance and cultivation of learning communities.

I will comment on three basic tools that are likely in your kit now. (Actually four as I explain below.) I dare to say, however, that these tools may well have gathered quite a bit of rust. Let's consider how to shine them up for more effective use ***to identify and cultivate character, courage, calling, and capability.***

Tool # 1 – Investigating References and Track Records ...

I almost wrote in the above caption what many organizations actually do in this regard; i.e. I almost wrote, "reference checking." "Checking" is woefully inadequate to describe the degree of scrutiny that needs to be done if one is to determine the depth and strength of a prospective leader's character, courage, calling, and capability.

For example, the "track records" provided by the candidate are often taken without corroboration. If your investigation lacks the diligence it needs to ensure information is relevant, reliable, and true then your risk of making the "wrong" choice is higher.

There are three places to polish on this rusty tool:

1. Selection of References;
2. Logistics of Data Collection; and,
3. Questions and Interview Technique.

1. Selection of References...

It is logical to expect that prospective candidates will show talent enlistment personnel the best portfolio that they can produce. There are even consultants that one can hire to help produce portfolios with resume, references, photos, and charts to impress decision makers.

Given the resources available to help a serious candidate impress decision makers, it is incumbent on recruiters to investigate them rigorously. Moreover, you should direct your investigation at references that are best positioned to give evidence to the depth of your prospective leader's character, courage, calling, and competency.

Take control. Establish prequalification criteria for both references and track records (accomplishments). If you don't do this the risk of getting inaccurate, incomplete, or useless information is high. Moreover, candidates may well (innocently or not) provide references that don't know them well.

Think about it. Would a prospective candidate knowingly give you a reference to investigate who will say negative things about them? Worse, if the candidate were of questionable character, he or she would even try to set up a situation where a search committee would get nothing but glowing reports. Would you, for example, accept everything written by someone on LinkedIn without verifying that information as complete and true? I know of people who have been dismissed for cause (fired for legally defendable reason) and yet they have an awesome resume on the web!

I am not rejecting the idea of using a reference provided by a candidate. Indeed, that is one source of names for your interrogation - oops, I meant to write investigation. (Or did I?) In any case, the main point is to prequalify prospective references; i.e. make sure you talk to or survey people who truly know your candidate and who can honesty provide you with relevant information.

Think like a detective. Plan your "enquiry" to get relevant, reliable, and accurate information about the prospect.

Common sense is your best friend here. For example, let's say that you want to hire an executive responsible for all the administrative functions of your organization, including its money. You'll want someone who can lead by example. They would need to have impeccable integrity and have a record of prudent stewardship. They will have to be able to work well with people. Look for some qualities of what Jim Collins terms level 5 leadership. Honesty and trustworthiness are essential. Do they have the courage to consistently tell the truth?

Recall too the notion in the previous chapter that true courage had right partners. When looking at a leader candidate's capacities for courage search out his or her intimacy with the "partners of courage" (wise, patient, humble). Also find out about the candidate's leadership style; partners of courage reside near level 5 leaders. Ask the questions, "Who should I talk to in order to access how he or she works with colleagues, both supervisors and subordinates? Who would know whether he or she is truly humble, patient, and wise? Who can I find who would know this candidate more intimately and thus be able to comment on such qualities as courage and calling?"

Now it is coming together.

Asking such common sense questions will lead you to develop a good prospect list of references for follow up. Obviously the list cannot be too long or you'll not likely have the resources to follow through. However, you will want to interview a sufficient number of references to get the information that you need to make a good decision.

Similarly, assessment of a candidate's achievements can follow the same logic. Often you'll find, for example, that level 5 leaders will underestimate their achievements because of their habit of ascribing credit to others.

Again, find the right people and ask the right questions if you seek right information.

2. *Determine the Logistics of Collecting Information …*

The logistics of collecting information is your next challenge. Face to face is obviously the best form of communication followed by telephone. If the latter needs to be used then see if Skype or another form of videoconference is available. Surveys have their place as well but need good skills of interpretation.

Again, think like a detective. If you find the candidate is using other people's accomplishments to bolster their own reputation, for example, then you probably have enough information on their character to give a failing, or at least questionable, grade.

So, consider your resources and then do your best to finalize a plan to collect relevant, reliable, and accurate information on your prospective candidate.

3. Questions and Interview Technique to solicit information on Character, Courage, Calling, and Competency of a Prospective Leader…

Even when you identify references that are genuine, you may not be able to collect information that you need for a good decision if questions are off target. Again, buddy up to your friend common sense and start to formulate questions intent on eliciting the relevant information.

While common sense gets you on the right track to formulate relevant questions, you will need practice to ask the questions in such a way as to elicit a useful response. Getting help from people who make their living from questions and questioning technique would be useful. Professional executive search experts can be asked to help. They would often volunteer their services. Don't laugh, but why not ask a detective or prosecuting lawyer to come and talk to your HR people? And/or, perhaps the CEO and management team can watch a TV show over lunch where the actor cast as detective has good questioning technique. While these ways to build up your competency in asking relevant questions are more fun than asking Google, you will find countless articles and books on the very subjects of interviewing and interview questions if you search.

This is professional development in action…enjoy!

A qualification…perhaps or perhaps not…

You might properly point out that I opened this section by stating that every person who is engaged in enlisting persons into an organization should have training in using this tool. But, you may say, a program officer who just wants to hire a part-time gymnastics coach can't be bothered with the time and effort to prepare a list of prospective references and follow up with investigation.

The latter statement would only be correct in the sense that one need not "over investigate" a prospective leader.

However, due diligence is still a smart mantra. Recall the Guidance Control Systems mentioned earlier in this chapter. Management will need to write guidelines appropriate to guide enlistment and provide training for line staff to comply with those guidelines. The principle that you need to know who you are hiring remains true. Just because an enlistment is part-time or volunteer doesn't negate the fact that they are performing an important activity to help you realize your mission. Thus, anyone in your organization responsible for recruitment of personnel at any level needs to spend sufficient time to research the background of a recruit or you risk the good reputation of the organization.

What if, for example, you go ahead and hire that coach purely on the basis of unstructured conversations and the impressive portfolio of credentials they present. Then, some time later, you handle complaints of that coach's inabilities or, worse, face a policeman following up a child molestation charge? Need I say more?

So, take the time before the hire to know who it is that you are enlisting or run the risk of spending more time later trying to manage a crisis and mend the tear in the good reputation of your organization.

Tool # 2 - Personality Assessments in Search of the 4 Essential Attributes...

Personality assessments are very useful tools in combination with other information that you are collecting. There are different ones to choose from and you don't need to look for the most expensive to get the one suitable for you.

While there are numerous brands and variations on the market, personality assessments or inventories fall into two broad types; one, DISC, which are intent on measuring the four key elements that influence behaviour styles, i.e. Dominance, Influence, Steadiness, and Competence; and, two, MBTI or Myers-Briggs Type Indicator. Take some of these tests yourself, read about them, and talk to those who have used them effectively. This will give you personal experience and useful insights as to how this tool can be of benefit.

There are numerous articles and books written by clinical practitioners, academics, and researchers that can help you better understand personality assessment. One book that I highly recommend based on actual cases is "The Performance Factor – Unlocking the Secrets of Teamwork," by Pat MacMillan. As the title suggests, the bulk of the book shares secrets of nurturing teamwork within your organization. In and of itself this is incredibly beneficial. Within those secrets, however, MacMillan reveals how to effectively use personality inventories for both individuals and teams. It is a must read for social sector leaders, in my view.

Moreover, I strongly propose that when searching for an appropriate personality assessment that you make sure to "assess the assessor" to ensure that they have a good track record. Honesty is important. The assessor needs to give you the honest facts and good reason why their test can benefit your organization.

Ask for some references and do give them a call. Use your newfound skills of investigation! Clients of assessors are less likely to give you the brochure version of their services.

Don't forget that as you work with this instrument (and the consultant teaching on its use) that you remember fours words - Character, Courage, Calling, and Capability. Talk to your expert consultant and discover how to bring these attributes out in the assessments.

This is a multipurpose tool…

Assessment tools are certainly useful for recruitment but they are also very helpful in building teams, cultivating learning organizations, and creating professional development plans. They are good investments in my view but as they normally have a cost associated with them you'll want to consider what positions require candidates to be assessed.

I realize that charities and non-profits are very cost sensitive. Many executives and aspiring executives may well have had one or more assessments done already. When recruiting, free to ask them for a copy and even have them interpret the results for you.

I trust that this tool is now polished and ready to be put into your toolkit. Before signing off on personality assessments and their usefulness in identifying and nurturing the four essential attributes of leaders I will share a couple of experiences that highlight the same principle.

"Getting into the Feet" of prospective leader candidates ...

I assume that readers are familiar with the meaning of the English idiom "walking in another's shoes." For the uninitiated it means that you can't really understand someone or identify with their hardship unless you can "walk in their shoes" for a time or distance.

Robert A. Evans of Plowshares Institute who, along with his wife Alice Frazer Evans, led a number of training workshops on the general topics of peace, reconciliation, and community transformation for my former organization. They talked about experiences in South Africa where locals used the expression "getting into another's feet!"

If you really want to know a prospective candidate you'll want to spend some time with people who have actually walked closely with them.

For example, talk with the secretary of the executive you are considering to hire or the board member you are considering to recommend. After you break the ice and earn their trust ask them a few personal questions about the prospect; for example, if their boss pays for their own personal stamps, if they eat out a lot on company expenses, and other such matters of accepting advantages of position. Check with colleagues of the prospective staff or board member to assess how they responded to situations of hardship and temptation. If, for example, they were not willing to expose wrongdoing for fear of personal reprisal then courage and strength of character are brought into question.

Get "into their feet" as best you can. The information that you glean will be most useful in recruitment decision-making and also for developing the character and leadership potential of your people.

Finally, a very brief personal story, if I may, to emphasize the same key principle of understanding people.

"A good name is more desirable than riches" (Proverbs 22:1) …

I credit my transition into a new culture and task of leading a major NPO to a senior colleague who, unbeknownst to me at the time, was my mentor. I met once a week for coffee with him. One day he said, "Chuck, you should have a Chinese name." "Ok," I said, "That sounds good, what do you suggest." He responded, "Let me think about it for a while."

Well, "a while," turned out to be a couple of months! I thought he had forgotten about it. Then, one morning at our weekly coffee he handed me a piece of paper with my three-character Chinese name.

My mentor then disclosed that the name should not only sound like my English name but also it should reflect my personality and character. I accepted his proposal. Pronounced in Putonghua, my Chinese name is "Xia Li Xin." In Cantonese it sounds similar to Allison (Ha Lei Sun).

He explained that "Ha / Xia" means summer, but, he elaborated to say that it symbolized the warmth I showed to people and the passion for work (i.e. warm/hot); "Lei / Li" means truth and reason; and, "Sun / Xin" connotes trust or trustworthiness.

I didn't fully appreciate then the effort that my mentor had put into what I thought was a straightforward exercise.

He took the time to work with and understand me before coming up with a name. He wanted the name to communicate the essence of my character. I am thankful for the time he took to determine my name and also for the knowledge and wisdom that he passed on during our meetings.

A Good Name

I can't even begin to count how many comments that I have received over the years concerning my "good" Chinese name. In real life one needs to be disciplined and constantly work at developing and maintaining a "good name." I encourage leaders, particularly young aspiring leaders, to **resist at all costs** any actions that will detract from your good name.

A good reputation for an individual or organization is awfully hard to gain and incredibly easy to loose. Be diligent and guard it with prudence and wisdom.

Tool # 3 (& # 4) – Performance Appraisals and Professional Development ...

It is common for organizations to have some form of performance appraisal. The range of their effectiveness, however, varies a lot – quite a lot.

I can imagine some readers cringing as we consider this topic. From my own experience, that cringing is largely because they picture a "scorecard" or "report card" approach to performance appraisal ("PA") with the person being appraised having little or no input. Regardless of management's idealistic goals and training efforts, the process generally reverts to the supervisor reading the verdict to the person being appraised. Moreover, HR may have already advised the supervisors of their quota of As or Bs (or whatever scoring system is used) so even good performers may get a lower grade than they deserve so as to fit into the theoretical bell curve and budget constraints. Cringe and cringe again.

Moreover, on the best practice checklist for a governing

board is one that asks for an evaluation of the Board's performance. Well, not much cringing here, as it is likely to be read, filed away, and never implemented.

I too was a cringer and avoider, and confess to not looking nearly hard enough to find people and organizations that were able to get positive results from appraisals and evaluations. However, I do remember numerous people voicing their views of the inadequacy of their PA process and the pain and agony it inflicted. Some of these voices were from faculty of esteemed academic institutions and executives from industry. Given the harm many PA processes inflict, I recall some of these learned people seriously questioning why their organization felt it necessary to conduct them at all!

Wow, given those reactions, we do indeed need to ask the question, why conduct performance appraisals? I now hear cringing from finance and administrative personnel as they wonder on what basis to award that half a percentage point salary increase!

On the other hand, social sector leaders tend to love coaching and helping people achieve their personal and professional goals. Why then is there so much cringing when they need to conduct a PA?

Well, before simply giving up and tossing this tool in the trash, let's do some serious cleaning and see if we can polish it for good working order.

The root of the problem may well be whether our appraisals taste and look like Salad or Chop Suey…

I have observed that administrators try to mix too many ingredients into a PA exercise, some of which are not complementary. What starts as a lovely fresh green salad with light dressing where one can taste all the individual ingredients and savour their enhanced flavour migrates to a recipe where ingredients get mashed together, stirred, and cooked. Before we realize it, the flavour of the lovely green salad with all its delicious individual ingredients is gone. The mixing and cooking has caused a whole new menu item to appear. Some may like it but, as we hear from many voices, others eat it purely because they must do so to survive.

Perhaps you can think of a better analogy but I feel many leaders allow their lovely "PA Salad" to turn into "PA Chop Suey" simply because there are too many things in the mix and the process creates such intense heat that it ends up cooking the life out of your people.

If your PA looks and tastes more like chop suey than fresh green salad, try changing the recipe and preparation to this:

1. Separate the ingredients of your performance appraisal ("PA") and professional development ("PD") dishes (i.e. treat performance appraisals and professional development sessions differently);
2. Now reconsider what you want to identify as performance and how you intend to evaluate it;
3. Similarly, how do you want your people to develop professionally and what action plan can you design and implement to get them there; and,
4. Revise the entire system to align with the performance objectives and development goals that you identified in recipe items 2 and 3.

Hopefully everyone will agree there are marked differences between PA and PD and you can work toward a new system. For example, let's have a listen to a meeting called by a senior HR executive of a hotel chain assigned by the CEO of the group to head up the task.

Attendees of the preliminary meeting: EF (HR exec as facilitator); CS (Common Sense); and BK (Business Knowledge).

EF breaks the ice and explains the task then asks BK, "Can you tell us what your performance indicators are?"

"Sure," says BK, "They are: occupancy rate, average room rate, yield, corporate account use rate, return guest rate, guest satisfaction response, travel advisor rating, and…"

"Ok, ok, slow down a bit. That's enough for now, thank you," says EF, "I am taking notes. Good, thanks. Let's come back to that later." EF turns to CS.

"CS, can you comment on how we might measure these?"

"Sure, that is easy," says CS. "You have computer software that tabulates and gives reports on many of the indices that BK gave plus you can collect data from different surveys to measure guest satisfaction."

"Thank you CS," EF said anticipating moving to another subject before CS added, "And you can design and conduct your own surveys too in order to get information on other performance indicators."

"Such as," said EF and she glanced over at BK.

"Such as how consistently clean the room attendant keeps the room and how many minutes on average he or she takes to clean it to standard," said CS before adding, "And how personable and helpful the receptionist is on check-in, and…"

EF politely stopped CS as she could see BK fidgeting. "Let's chart what we have identified thus far," said EF, "And then we'll dialogue some more and see if there are other important indices that we want to identify for tracking as performance targets."

"Allow me to correct your semantics EF," said BK respectfully, "We can develop a comprehensive list of performance indices and ways to measure them but to actually set targets we need the participation of other managers. Moreover, we need to determine whether the targets are for a team or for an individual."

"Quite right," responds EF, "Let's review our notes and wrap up our discussion on performance indices and measurements for the time being. We can then reconvene when I find a time that other colleagues can join."

The meeting adjourns and EF reports to the CEO.

I think that you get the idea. The discussion and dialogue (two different things) were restricted to indices that hotels use to assess their performance, and to ways and means of measuring those indices. The matters of training and development of individuals and teams were not on the agenda. Why? Because the exercise of identifying meaningful performance indices, discovering accurate ways to measure them, and finally setting reasonably achievable targets is quite involved and complex in and of itself. If leaders can discipline themselves to evaluate performance within relevant, clear, and manageable parameters then they have a good chance at enjoying a delicious fresh green salad.

There are two primary targets for performance plans and appraisals; operations (all efforts to further mission, including administrative); and, governance (board of directors).

Professional development…

PD has different objectives than PA. You cannot measure a person's development professionally by the same criteria as performance; e.g. occupancy rates or yields. Wait, I hear some cringing again.

Yes, I agree there can be a correlation between PD and competency and thus the contribution that an individual or team has on performance indicators but these are not easy to identify or measure, and they can be impacted by external variables.

An extreme example of the latter truth was the time when the WHO (World Health Organization) listed Hong Kong on a travel alert because of the SARS virus. Overnight, occupancies in hotels plummeted. It was high season and many hotels had well over 90 % in advance reservations. Within a few days many were lucky to achieve 10 %. I was CEO of an organization that operated a 365-room hotel. Frankly, we had a lot more to worry about than a performance appraisal but if we had done so at that time our results would be disastrous. However, our business philosophy and PD efforts to support them did not change. In fact, we got a chance to teach others of our approach due to this unusual circumstance. (But that is another story.)

This example shows how outside variables can cause a gap between individual and team performance and actual outcomes. There are many such variables that influence performance targets, including financial, political, and environmental. Conversely, when all the negative variables become positive, a hotel with poorly trained and performing staff can still realize incredibly high occupancy rates (but likely not customer return rates).

More clarification ...

PD indicators are very much linked to business philosophy and the way an organization conducts their activities. They are very different indicators than performance indicators but are of fundamental importance to the mission and reputation of the organization.

For example, Hotel A takes the view that it wants a reputation that it is safe and clean with friendly, knowledgeable service. Hotel B is content to deal with a few complaints of theft, mold, and unfriendly staff. Hotel A invests a good deal and time and money in training, supervision, and other PD programs. Hotel B gets by with basic training and supervision. But, low and behold, they both get 90 % occupancy in high season with pretty good yields. In fact Hotel B's yields are higher because of their low payroll.

Get the idea? Performance wise, from indicators such as occupancy and yield, Hotel B might just outperform Hotel A. But, what of long-term goals of high standards and good reputation? I think that you can assume that A will still continue to invest in professional development for its employees.

Therefore, separate performance assessment from professional development. Link performance to indicators that reflect targeted achievement or outputs and link development to how you choose to deliver service and build reputation. Your people will be more satisfied in their work and your organization will advance toward a genuine learning community.

Time to Start Cultivating

The above practices and tools are quite sufficient to get you started at cultivating effective and sustainable learning organizations. I am sure that you'll add tools to your kit in due course.

Before cultivating in earnest, however, take some time to carefully and prayerfully prepare your plan. You'll want to be able to discern between your healthy plants and weeds that intend to choke them. Enlisting leaders of integrity who are called to the work in which you are engaged and who have the courage and capacity to accept the call and work diligently with others is your ultimate goal. If such people in both governing and operational roles surround a CEO then the road toward becoming a great organization is smooth and sure.

Enjoy the fruits of your labour.

Books and Work by Scholars Referenced

Alice Frazer Evans and Robert A. Evans with Ronald S. Kraybill, "Peace Skills; A Manual For Community Mediators and A Leaders' Guide," (JOSSEY-BASS San Francisco, California), 2001

Gordon T. Smith, "Courage and Calling – Embracing Your God Given Gifts," (InterVarsity Press, Downers Grove, Illinois), 1st Edition 1999

Jim Collins, "Good To Great And The Social Sectors; A Monograph to Accompany the Book Good to Great," (Jim Collins, Boulder Colorado), 2005

Jim Collins, "Level 5 Leadership: The Triumph of Humility and Fierce Resolve," (An Article in The Harvard Business Review's HBR OnPoint: 5831), 2001

Peter M. Senge, "The Fifth Discipline – The Art & Practice of The Learning Organization," (New York: Doubleday), 1990

Pat MacMillan, "The Performance Factor – Unlocking the Secrets of Teamwork," (Broadman & Holman Publishers, Nashville, Tennessee), 2001

The Bible – The Message and New International Versions

About the Author

Chuck Allison worked with the Young Men's Christian Association for 35 years. He served with four different YMCAs in Canada in 10 years. In 1986 he and his family moved to Hong Kong in response to an invitation to join the YMCA in that remarkable city. Within four months of moving there he was appointed General Secretary (CEO) of YMCA of Hong Kong, a post that he held until December 2010. His position provided him opportunity to apply the leadership principles of which he writes in this book to cultivate a substantial organization that ranked as one of the most resourceful YMCA's in the world. This vantage point also allowed him to witness first hand the tremendous social transformation in China and other Asian countries.

He now resides in Langley, BC, Canada. His interest remains with the personal and professional development of aspiring leaders of teams and organizations.

CPSIA information can be obtained at www.ICGtesting.com
Printed in the USA
LVOW05s0037071114

412205LV00005B/35/P